Impressionist Masterpieces
at the Jeu de Paume, Paris

Impressionist Masterpieces at the Jeu de Paume, Paris

Foreword by Michel Laclotte

Inspector-General of French Museums,
Chief Curator at the Musée du Louvre (Paintings)
and the Musée d'Orsay, Paris

Introduction by Edward Lucie-Smith

Commentaries on the plates by Anne Distel
Claire Frèches-Thory
Sylvie Gache-Patin
Geneviève Lacambre

Curators at the Musée d'Orsay, Paris

With 73 color plates

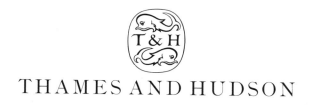

THAMES AND HUDSON

Foreword and commentaries translated from the French by
Edward Lucie-Smith

Photographs supplied by the Musées nationaux, Paris

First published in the USA in 1984 by Thames and Hudson Inc.,
500 Fifth Avenue, New York, New York 10110

Library of Congress Catalog Card Number 83–50638

Color reproduction by Cliché Lux S.A., La Chaux-de-Fonds, Switzerland
Printed and bound in the Netherlands by Royal Smeets Offset b.v.

CONTENTS

FOREWORD

The history of the national collection of Impressionist painting, now to be seen at the Jeu de Paume museum, goes back to 1890, when Claude Monet organized a public subscription for the purchase of Manet's *Olympia* for the Musée du Luxembourg (then the official repository of modern art in Paris), fearing that otherwise it might be lost to France and go to the United States. Two years later, the state bought Renoir's *Jeunes filles au piano* from the artist. But coming as they did after years of indifference or hostility on the part of the establishment – attitudes shared by many collectors and critics – these acquisitions were not as yet real signs of official recognition. Although the Caillebotte bequest in 1895, which included masterpieces by Manet, Renoir, Cézanne, Sisley, Monet and Pissarro, was not in fact refused altogether, as legend still has it, only part of it was accepted.

The International Exhibition of 1900 marked the end of systematic opposition from the administrators of the arts, though the artists connected with the Salon and their supporters remained unreconciled to Impressionism and Post-Impressionism. Even so, a subscription organized in 1900, to acquire Gauguin's *D'où venons nous? Que sommes nous? Où allons nous? (Where Have We Come From? What Are We? Where Are We Going?)* for the Musée du Luxembourg was a failure, and the painting is now in Boston. For its formation, the national collection was forced to rely on private generosity. In 1906, Etienne Moreau-Nélaton gave, among other masterpieces, Manet's *Le déjeuner sur l'herbe*, and in 1911 Isaac de Camondo bequeathed a splendid series of works by Degas, Monet and Cézanne, as well as the collection's first Van Gogh.

Thereafter, this basic collection was augmented by a flow of acquisitions. There were gifts from the families of artists (Toulouse-Lautrec in 1902; Bazille in 1904 and 1924; Renoir in 1923; Monet in 1927; Pissarro in 1930); purchases from the Degas sale of 1917; and above all there were gifts from well-informed and generous collectors (May, Kœchlin, Pellerin, David-Weill, Rouart, Goujon, Gangnat, du Cholet, Quinn), and also from the Friends of the Musée du Luxembourg. The Personnaz bequest of 1937 was the last major acquisition before the war.

Today, we cannot but regret the fact that substantial funds for large-scale purchasing were not available in the inter-war period. They would have made it possible for France to retain a number of masterpieces from an artistic movement which, though misunderstood for so long, has now taken its proper place in history.

The light-filled Jeu de Paume museum in the Tuileries was first opened in 1947. The opening took place at a time when artists were enraptured by the idea of pure painting, and it signalled the popular triumph of Impressionism. An active purchasing policy could at long last be put in hand, and an attempt made to fill the gaps in the collection – Seurat, for example – while this was still possible. Once again collectors, and the Society of Friends of the Louvre (to which the Jeu de Paume belonged), provided effective help. There were gifts of single major works by Cézanne, Van Gogh, Gauguin and Renoir. Groups of paintings were given by important collectors such as Polignac, Charpentier, Laroche, Gourgaud, Lung, Bernheim, Halphen, Goldschmidt-Rothschild, Meyer and Kahn-Sriber, who reserved part of their collections for the Louvre. Entire collections were also donated (Gachet, 1951–54; Mollard, 1972; Kaganovitch, 1973), each reflecting not only the taste of their particular owner, but also that of an entire generation. The Jeu de Paume collection grew in another way as well, through the fact that important works of art could now be ceded in lieu of estate duties. This added some major works, among them Renoir's *La danse à la ville* and Monet's *Rue Montorgueil*, in 1978 and 1982 respectively.

Although the Jeu de Paume provided an ideal setting at the time of its opening, the building in the Tuileries is now stretched almost beyond its capacity, and it is no longer possible to exhibit the collection as it should ideally be seen, so greatly has it been enlarged over the years. (But who indeed could seriously complain about such expansion?) Nor is the building now spacious enough to cope with the ever greater numbers of visitors. Already Seurat and Toulouse-Lautrec have gone to join the other Neo-Impressionists and the Nabis in the Palais de Tokyo. In a few years, the Impressionists from the Jeu de Paume and the Post-Impressionists from the Palais de Tokyo will be reunited in a new museum now being built: the Musée d'Orsay. There they will no longer be viewed in isolation. Instead, it will be possible to compare them with work done by other artists at the same epoch. Undoubtedly, the Musée d'Orsay will provide a richer, more balanced and comprehensive view of late nineteenth-century art. Yet it is equally certain that those who have experienced the brilliance of Impressionism at the Jeu de Paume have experienced a joy which it is impossible to forget.

MICHEL LACLOTTE

INTRODUCTION

The Jeu de Paume was built as an orangery and takes its present name from the *jeu de paume*, or real tennis court, fitted up by Napoleon III in 1862 for the use of his son, the ill-fated Prince Imperial. Its role as a museum of Impressionism began as recently as 1947, and it says something for the impact made by the collections housed there that its name has become not merely world-famous but synonymous with the kind of art housed within its walls – perhaps the most popular and accessible school of art ever to have existed. More than this, the Jeu de Paume belongs to a very small group among the major museums of the world in which a particular kind of art can be experienced with an intensity available nowhere else. In this respect it resembles the Acropolis Museum in Athens, the only place where a visitor can feel the full impact of Late Archaic Greek sculpture. But unlike many other major museums – for example, its neighbour the Louvre – the Jeu de Paume's collections are not inexhaustibly enormous, and it is possible to grasp a great deal of what it has to offer on a single visit.

Impressionism marks a crisis-point in nineteenth-century art – not merely the abandonment of many ideas which had until then seemed immutably established, but the beginning of many attitudes that we still recognize as being modern and immediately relevant to ourselves. At the same time, the Impressionist movement did not spring up suddenly and in total isolation from the historical process. It is not too much to claim that French art had in one way or another been preparing for its appearance ever since the early years of the eighteenth century. Although Impressionism's immediate ancestors were the realists and naturalists of the mid-nineteenth century, its remoter ones included not only Delacroix but Watteau, Boucher, Fragonard and (gazing across the Pyrenees) a number of great Spanish masters, notably Velásquez and Goya. To insist that Impressionism is an art concerned with nothing but the immediate sensation is at best a half-truth and at worst an extremely serious error.

Yet the concern felt by the Impressionists for this immediate sensation, for the uncensored truth of the eye, conveyed without either forethought or afterthought, is something which did undoubtedly exist. When the senior painters who afterwards formed part of the group began to try to make their careers in the 1860s, during the last decade of the Second Empire, realism had already established itself as a way of seeing opposed to the conventional academic style favoured by the entrenched Salon juries. This impulse towards a less conventional way of seeing affected artists who were themselves deeply conservative by temperament. We meet with interesting examples in the early work of Degas, for instance in his painting of *La famille Bellelli*, which dates from 1858–60. Here there is a new attitude to composition, evidently inspired by photography – one of the many scientific inventions of the period. These inventions, added together, were completely to alter man's perception of the world, and the Impressionists were the first artists to make a fundamental response to the change.

When Daguerre announced the perfection of his invention in 1839, enthusiasm for it spread like wildfire, because the nineteenth-century bourgeois public had already anticipated, and with some impatience, a democratization of the whole image-making process. What fascinated early enthusiasts for photography was not merely the notion that nature could now be persuaded to make her own portrait (the camera lens was deemed to be an entirely objective means of recording reality), but that photographic plates captured that reality with a fidelity and a regard for detail hitherto unattainable. The one thing that early photographs lacked, and it was a major omission, was colour.

The nature of colour, and the way in which the human eye perceived it, had naturally enough also attracted the scientific curiosity of the nineteenth century, and the Impressionist masters were the first artists to put the scientists' discoveries into effect. The conclusion of the theorists was that the whole gamut of colours derived in fact from a few pure tones, which blended optically on the retina. It became the ambition of the Impressionist group to demonstrate the truth of this contention by painting in small, pure touches that coalesced to create the required hue only when the spectator stood at a certain distance from the canvas. And in order to achieve a perfect reproduction of what the eye really perceived, the Impressionists believed that pictures were, as far as possible, to be created in the open air, in the very presence of what the artist was depicting.

If this had been all there was to it, the Impressionists would have remained purely a school of landscape painters. And indeed, as the visitor to the Jeu de Paume will see, landscape subjects do loom very large in their total output. Certain members of the group, notably Alfred Sisley, produced virtually nothing else. It may be unconventional to begin a survey of Impressionist aims with Sisley instead of with greater and more all-encompassing masters such as Manet and Monet, but there is real reason for doing so. Sisley's beautiful *L'inondation à Port-Marly*, painted in 1876, and one of the very finest of all his pictures, shows the close link between Impressionism and somewhat earlier practitioners of *plein air* landscape painting such as Corot. The treatment of the house on the left is very much in Corot's manner, even though the floodwaters themselves are treated with a much broader and more glittering touch. A picture done two years earlier, Sisley's *Le brouillard* of 1874, because of the very nature of its subject, gives a notion of the extremes to which the Impressionists could take their particular view of landscape. The painting seems at first sight to be almost without structure, a capricious piling up of variously coloured dots. What one has here is not a painting of a particular spot, but an attempt to capture a particular effect of light. The locality of the painting is irrelevant. So is the idea of trying to convey intellectual content as opposed to physical sensation.

This line of thinking was to be carried to extremes by Claude Monet in the latter part of his career. One of Monet's innovations was to paint the same motif over and over again. There are long series devoted to the west façade of Rouen Cathedral (two examples are illustrated in this book), to a group of haystacks in a field, and to the waterlilies which filled the ponds in the garden Monet created for himself at Giverny. The Jeu de Paume, which previously lacked one of these late paintings of waterlilies, has recently been fortunate enough to fill the gap with a splendid example.

Monet may have chosen Rouen Cathedral as the subject for one of these series with polemical intent, since here was a major Gothic structure infused with a wide range of meanings for all Frenchmen, and indeed for all Europeans who might see it. But these meanings were something the painter simply chose to ignore. He was intent only on recording the permutations of light and atmosphere on the complex façade, whose sole function was to modulate the atmospheric flux and make it visible. The Impressionist obsession with analysis of light and the process of seeing becomes the be-all and end-all of art; everything else is pushed aside as an irrelevance. And this of course implies a view of the world and of the painter's role in it that would have seemed not only outrageous but actually incomprehensible when Monet first began to paint, at Le Havre under Boudin's tuition, towards the end of the 1850s.

Monet's studies of *La cathédrale de Rouen* are of especial importance because they are the clearest demonstration of the way in which Impressionism altered the morality of painting. Until the middle of the nineteenth century, it had been a universally agreed idea that art was meant to express some moral standpoint espoused by the artist. This notion informs even the work of Gustave Courbet, the great mid-century realist who preceded the Impressionists and who had occasioned so much controversy among French art critics and the public. Impressionism changed all this. It declared morals in paintings to be irrelevant, yet at the same time it turned the actual practice of painting into a series of moral choices: the painter had to be completely true to his own feelings concerning the nature of art. It is this conviction which links two artists otherwise as different from one another as Monet and Cézanne.

The question of morality and the painter's attitude to it is also extremely relevant in the case of Manet, who otherwise seems to fit rather uneasily into the Impressionist group. The Jeu de Paume is fortunate enough to possess, amongst a superlative group of paintings by this artist, two works which were amongst the most controversial of their whole epoch: *Le déjeuner sur l'herbe* and *Olympia*, both painted in 1863. *Le déjeuner sur l'herbe* was described by an outraged contemporary critic as follows: 'A commonplace woman of the demi-monde, as naked as can be, shamelessly lolls between two dandies dressed to the teeth.' He went on to call the painting 'a young man's practical joke, a shameful open sore not worth exhibiting in this way.' The irony was that Manet had made use of the most approved classic sources – the composition derives directly from a Renaissance engraving by Marcantonio Raimondi, after Raphael, and is strongly reminiscent of Titian's *Concert champêtre*, then as now one of the glories of the Louvre. *Olympia*, a reclining nude indebted both to Goya's *Naked Maja* and Titian's *Venus of Urbino*, aroused an equivalent anger among conservative critics, who translated into social and moral terms their disapproval of Manet's technical radicalism – his reduction of gradations of tone, and his emphasis on outline and on the importance of the picture-plane. Manet was not at this stage experimenting with optical mixtures, though he painted magnificent *plein air* scenes in the course of his career – *Sur la plage*, of 1873, is a particularly beautiful example.

Sur la plage is also an example of something else: the Impressionists' ability to render the very texture of life in their time. This, even more than their brilliant freshness of colour, is the quality that has made them so firmly beloved by the public. A number of extremely familiar examples of this gift can be found in these pages – Manet's own *La serveuse de bocks*, Renoir's incomparable *Moulin de la Galette*, and most of all a whole series of paintings and pastels by Degas. Indeed, Degas was perhaps, among all the contributors to the various Impressionist exhibitions, the one most determined to reflect what he saw as the nature of contemporary life. Yet of all the major Impressionists he remains, I think, the one who is most often misunderstood by the public.

What attitude are we meant to take, for example, towards one of the best-known of all his versions of contemporary urban life, the *Au café* of 1876? Its alternative title, *L'absinthe*, suggests that this may be an exception among Impressionist pictures in having a directly moral purpose, and it is certainly one where any trace of *joie de vivre* seems to be absent – two melancholic figures seated side by side, their psychological distance from one another stressed by their physical proximity. Degas seems to imply a comment on the meaningless character of daily life. But the comment, if there is one, is made with sophisticated obliqueness. Degas is fascinated by the world of Parisian entertainment, but he sees it characteristically in terms of work – the players in *L'orchestre de l'Opéra* are men doing a job, oblivious to events on the stage. The members of *La classe de danse* are similarly preoccupied with what is for them labour, though for others it will become entertainment.

The Impressionists were not united in their political views. Degas' opinions were conservative, whereas Camille Pissarro was a Socialist, but their work is surprisingly eloquent about their commitment to the world as they found it. The delightful high-jinks of the Moulin de la Galette can be put against the background supplied not only by Degas' weary *Les repasseuses* but also against the smoke and grime of Monet's *La gare Saint-Lazare* and the frankly industrial quality of Pissarro's view of *Le port de Rouen, Saint-Sever*. All these works express the conviction that painting must come out of ordinary life, and continue to march in step with it.

Pissarro is perhaps the most difficult to characterize of all the Impressionists, and there are some signs, particularly his venture into a more systematic kind of Neo-Impressionism under the influence of Seurat (see, for instance, his *Femme dans un clos ... Eragny*), which indicate that he found it difficult to characterize himself. It is, in fact, in Pissarro's œuvre that we sometimes glimpse some of the losses as well as the gains in Impressionism's determination to eschew any kind of moral message. Pissarro's noble, thoughtful *Self-portrait* of 1873 gives us more than a glimpse of a nature which all his colleagues respected for its generosity and gentleness. And the charming *Jeune fille à la baguette* shows Pissarro's secret hankering for a kind of art which Impressionist doctrine seemed to make impossible – the profoundly touching peasant scenes of J. F. Millet. But Pissarro himself is never able to achieve the kind of resonance which Millet reaches. To be sure, his finest landscapes, like the *Entrée du village de Voisins*, are marvellously executed but still leave us with the feeling that there is something missing, some essential element of himself which the artist has been unable to express – though perhaps this is simply the hindsight that comes from knowing a certain amount about Pissarro's life.

It is interesting to remember, at any rate, that Millet was also a primary source for Vincent van Gogh, who is one of the three major Post-Impressionist painters (along with Cézanne and Gauguin) whose work is also exhibited at the Jeu de Paume. Van Gogh, however, is not perhaps the one with whom one would choose to start, if one wants to understand how Impressionist attitudes eventually came to seem constricting. The master one must turn to is Cézanne.

Cézanne spent a period of his career as an Impressionist painter in a strictly technical sense – he even showed in the Impressionist exhibitions of 1874 and 1877, which made him an official member of the group. At this stage he was chiefly influenced by Pissarro, whom he had known as early as 1862, when he worked at the Académie Suisse. The curious satirical work *Une moderne Olympia*, showing the squat balding artist goggling at the naked goddess uncovered for his inspection, may express some of the doubts that long plagued him. Cézanne only fully discovered his own method and his own potentialities in 1882, when he went to live at Aix-en-Provence. It was then that he seemingly abandoned Impressionist precepts in favour of their complete opposite. But in fact this abandonment is already becoming apparent in *La maison du pendu*, painted as early as 1873. And it is of course entirely visible in later work such as *Le vase bleu* and *Nature morte aux oignons*. These latter paintings are both classical examples of Cézanne's preoccupation with absolutely commonplace subject-matter, which he uses as the raw material for a stringent, immutable pictorial architecture having nothing to do with the impression made by the fleeting moment or a particular effect of light. Writing to Emile Bernard in 1904, Cézanne said:

The writer expresses himself by means of abstractions, whereas the painter concretises his sensations and perceptions in line and colour. One is not over-scrupulous, nor over-sincere, nor over-submissive to nature, but one has more or less mastered one's model, and above all one's means of expression. One must enter into the object one is observing and strive to express it in the most logical manner possible.

The full consequences of pursuing this doctrine to its logical conclusion can be seen in the great canvases of *Baigneurs*, painted between 1890 and 1900, and especially in the more drastic of two versions of this subject in the Jeu de Paume collection. Here one notes how the ostensible subject matter has become a mere pretext for the act of making a painting, which Cézanne sees in terms of a surface completely organized by means of colour and line, a statement sufficient to itself, without reference to anything outside.

If Cézanne depersonalizes art, the opposite is true of the work of Gauguin and Van Gogh. There are few artists where our knowledge of the biographical facts matters so much to our appreciation of what they do. Van Gogh did not encounter Impressionism first-hand until 1886, when he came to Paris to join his brother Theo, and his canvases touched by its influence do not reveal the full extent of his powers. In fact, if Impressionism based itself on the objective evaluation of appearance, and in particular of the effects of light, Van Gogh pursued an almost opposite line. His method was to project his own emotions on to what he saw. The famous canvas showing *La chambre de Van Gogh à Arles* is not simply a representation of a commonplace room but is instead a reflection of a highly charged state of feeling, symbolized both by the objects the room contains and by the way these objects, and indeed the very space they occupy, are depicted. The same is true of the later painting of *L'église d'Auvers-sur-Oise*, which was done in 1890, the year of Van Gogh's suicide, and which radiates the manic intensity of the artist's state of mind. One has only to imagine what Sisley or Pissarro might have made of the same subject to see how totally different Van Gogh's intentions are. His portraits, and especially his self-portraits, are similarly subjective, a search not so much for truth to physical appearances as for the spirit which lives within a man.

Van Gogh did not set out to found a school: Gauguin did. There was always in him something of the teacher and leader, and he adopted Impressionism (like Cézanne, he was introduced to it by Pissarro) only in order to reject it. Gauguin's real independence of Impressionism began with his first visit to Pont-Aven in Brittany in 1886, though the final break did not come until the following year, as a result of his contact with the young Emile Bernard, who was busy preaching the superiority of synthesis – the bringing together of all elements of an experience, subjective as well as objective – to the mere analysis of appearances, which is what Impressionism was all about.

The final stage of Gauguin's rejection of everything Impressionism stood for is marked by his departure for Tahiti in 1891, in search of a completely different world. The pictures he painted during his two residences in the South Seas – he returned to France in 1893 only to set out again in 1895 – are those which have fixed his image forever in the popular mind. Even though we know that Gauguin was guilty of fictionalizing what he found, the act of creating these Tahitian paintings, even in defiance of the facts, answered a pressing need within himself, and that was the point of producing them. The voyage to the South Seas was not as decisive as has been claimed. It is, for example, interesting to compare Gauguin's images of *luxe, calme et volupté* with certain late paintings by Renoir, most of all perhaps with the wonderful double nude *Les baigneuses*, which Renoir painted in 1918–19 at the very end of a long creative life. No more than Gauguin's South Sea beauties do these have anything to do with what the artist has actually observed. The pretence that appearances are being meticulously analysed (never very strong in Renoir's work) has long since been abandoned. What we get instead is a sensual hymn of praise for the richness offered by the life of the senses.

I suggested towards the beginning of this essay that the roots of Impressionism are at least partly to be found in the French eighteenth century. Renoir has a strong neo-rococo streak, itself very much in keeping with certain aspects of French late-nineteenth-century taste, and *Les baigneuses* certainly serves to reinforce the comparison – with nudes by Boucher, for example. But it also suggests a more general idea. The durable appeal of the Impressionists is not to be found simply in the sparkle of the typical Impressionist palette. It has also something to do with a fundamental rationality of attitude, a willingness to accept the nature of the world and to express a frank delight in its sensual surface. The *homme moyen sensuel* in most of us will return gratefully to a school which proved that it is one of the functions of art to make us see more intensely and perfectly what everyone is capable of perceiving. No painters ever fulfilled this function better than the Impressionist masters.

EDWARD LUCIE-SMITH

PLATES AND COMMENTARIES

The following abbreviations have been used for the authors' names:

AD   Anne Distel
CF-T   Claire Frèches-Thory
SG-P   Sylvie Gache-Patin
GL   Geneviève Lacambre

Frédéric BAZILLE (1841–1870)

L'atelier de Bazille (Bazille's Studio), 1869–70

Oil on canvas, $38\frac{5}{8} \times 50\frac{5}{8}$ (98 × 128.5)

Bequest of Marc Bazille, brother of the artist, 1924 (R.F. 2449)

Bazille, who came from a well-known family in Montpellier, was a friend of Bruyas, Courbet's patron. He arrived in Paris in 1862 and that autumn entered Gleyre's studio, where he became friendly with Monet, Renoir and Sisley. In the spring of 1863, these young artists, their enthusiasm fired by Manet's paintings shown at the Galerie Martinet and later by those at the Salon des Refusés (see p. 74), elected him as their leader. It is this group of friends which Bazille depicts here, at his studio in the Batignolles quarter of Paris, which he occupied from 1 January 1868 to 15 May 1870.

Once he had returned from the summer holidays of 1869, and had had black curtains put up which allowed him to paint without interruption, Bazille started work on several paintings. They included a studio interior and a female nude for the Salon – pictures which were to occupy him all winter. The female nude *La toilette* (*The Toilet*) (Musée de Montpellier) is depicted unfinished in this work, hanging above the sofa. It was rejected by the Salon of 1870. Also visible to the left is the *Pêcheur à l'epervier* (*Fisherman with a Net*), rejected in 1869. Behind the easel is the *Tireuse de cartes* (*The Fortune-teller*), while the large painting on the wall above the piano is *Terrasse de Méric* (*The Terrace at Méric*) of 1867 (Musée de Montpellier). Above the pianist (Edmond Maître, a friend of Bazille), a still-life by Monet is a reminder that Bazille helped the artist by buying his work, notably *Femmes au jardin* (see p. 88). On the easel is the *Vue de village* (*View of a Village*) of 1868 (Musée de Montpellier), which Manet is examining, hat on head. The artist had a profound influence on Bazille, as he himself acknowledged when he wrote to his father on 1 January 1870: 'Manet has made me what I am.' Bazille is the tall slim figure in the centre of the picture. The identification of the three figures to the left is less certain. It depends on two contradictory statements made by Monet, probably after the Bazille retrospective at the Salon d'Automne of 1910, where this picture was exhibited. Are we to identify the man next to Manet as Monet or Zacharie Astruc? And are those grouped to the left Renoir and Zola, or Monet and Sisley? These artists and writers were among Manet's admirers, and were depicted by Fantin-Latour at the same epoch in his *L'atelier des Batignolles* (*Studio at Batignolles*, Jeu de Paume). But, unlike Fantin-Latour, who remained faithful to the example of the Dutch masters, Bazille has produced a totally modern composition, which evokes the quasi-bourgeois atmosphere of the place where he liked to entertain his friends. His death in battle a few months later makes this work, painted for his own pleasure, a particularly moving testament.   GL

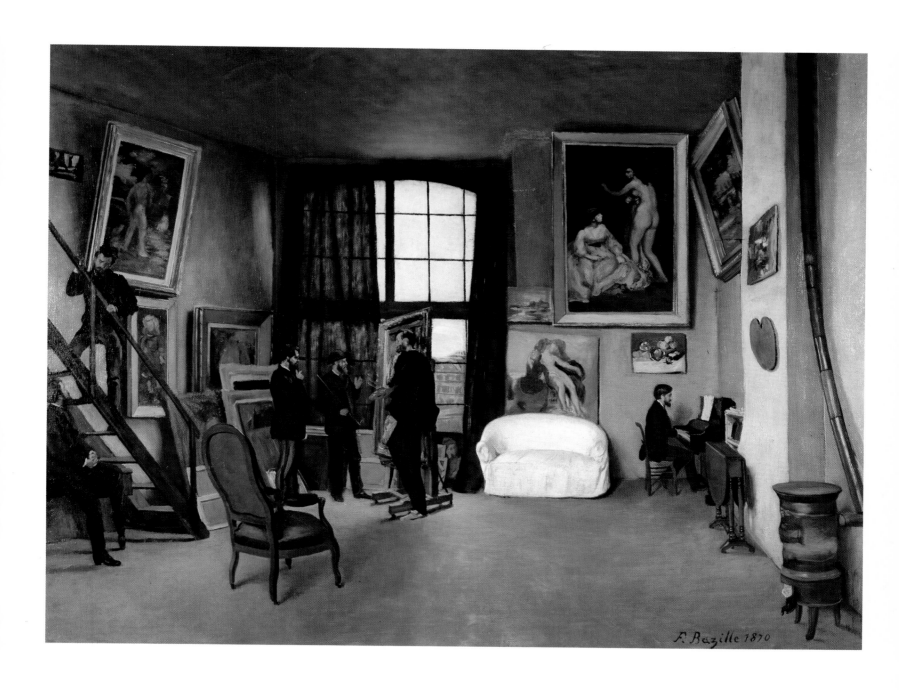

Eugène BOUDIN (1824–1898)

La plage de Trouville (*The Beach at Trouville*), 1864

Oil on panel, $10\frac{1}{4} \times 18\frac{1}{8}$ (26×48)

Gift of Eduardo Mollard, 1961 (R.F. 1961–26)

Boudin's début in the domain of art was a modest one, beginning as he did as a paper-merchant and framer at Le Havre, and using his shop to show work by painters such as Troyon and Millet who passed through the town. These men encouraged him to paint, and a grant from the town council enabled him to go and study in Paris in 1851. But he always remained faithful to the Normandy coast, where in 1858 he met Claude Monet, whose first teacher he became. He also got to know Courbet and Baudelaire; the latter was delighted with his sky studies, and supported him when he exhibited at the Salon for the first time in 1859 with an ambitious and relatively large work, *Le pardon de Sainte-Anne-la-Palud* (*The Pardon of Sainte-Anne-la-Palud*, now in the museum at Le Havre). The painting depicts a picturesque throng gathered round white tents and market-stalls exposed to the open air, all set in a wide blue landscape.

Certain elements from *Le pardon de Sainte-Anne-la-Palud* – among them the hill and the chapel with its bell-tower – occur again here in this delightful little painting of the beach at Trouville. To the right are the high slate roofs of a villa, and the hill behind the beach; in the centre are summer visitors, standing about, or seated on chairs, with brilliant white bathing cabins and two tall flag-poles in the background. All of this occupies only the bottom of a composition in which the sky occupies most of the space.

In the same year that this was painted, Boudin met Courbet and Manet at Trouville, which was then a smart watering-place. He had started to paint its bustling fashionable society in 1862, on the advice of Eugène Isabey, a member of the Barbizon School. In 1863 he depicted *L'impératrice Eugénie et sa suite à Trouville* (*The Empress Eugenie and Her Suite at Trouville*, Glasgow Museums and Art Galleries, Burrell Collection) in a dazzling swirl of crinolines, and submitted *La plage de Trouville* to the Salon in 1864.

Out of loyalty to his Impressionist friends, Boudin took part in the first Impressionist exhibition of 1874, but thereafter remained faithful to the Salon, which did not hold his temporary apostasy against him.

GL

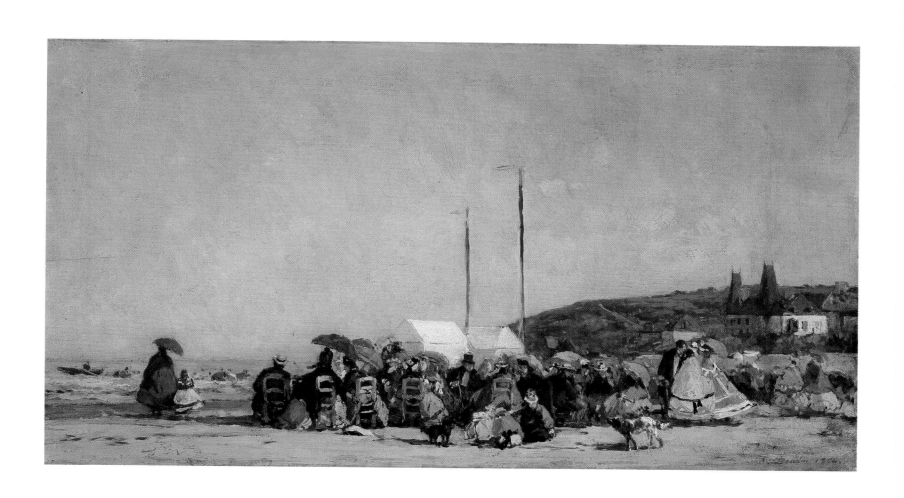

Gustave CAILLEBOTTE (1848–1894)

Voiliers à Argenteuil (*Sailing-boats at Argenteuil*), c. 1888

Oil on canvas, $25\frac{5}{8} \times 21\frac{5}{8}$ (65 × 55)

Purchased in 1954 (R.F. 1954–31)

Caillebotte came from an upper-middle-class family and inherited a substantial fortune on the death of his father in 1873, which allowed him to pursue his vocation as an artist. Having been a pupil of Bonnat, he entered the Ecole des Beaux-Arts in 1873, but left it early after his work was rejected by the Salon in 1875. It was probably through Degas, who was a friend of Bonnat, that he came into contact with the Impressionist group, then newly established. From 1876 onwards he participated in its exhibitions, playing an important part as organizer, but twice did not exhibit (in 1881 and 1886) after dissensions within the group.

His early work is characterized by a daring naturalism, taking urban life as its theme, but he returned deliberately to Impressionist methods in his brilliant Argenteuil period. He thus seemed old-fashioned, or at any rate lagging behind the times, when he exhibited his work in 1888 at Durand-Ruel's gallery, and with the Group of XX in Brussels where he showed paintings of boats on the Seine. Some, such as the one reproduced here, are expecially successful in the balance of their composition and evocation of the quality of light. Since 1882 Caillebotte had owned a house by the river, with a large flower-filled garden, at Le Petit-Gennevilliers, across the river from Argenteuil. He settled here permanently in 1887. The river bank and the landing-stage near his house appear in this picture, and on the horizon, behind the old wooden bridge at Argenteuil, are the supports of the railway bridge and the hills of Sanois and Orgemont.

Caillebotte is equally famous for the role he played as patron of his friends the Impressionists as he is as a painter – in fact in 1876 he made them beneficiaries of his first will. Thanks to him, many of their paintings entered the Musée du Luxembourg (then the museum of modern art in Paris) in 1896, despite both the refusal of part of his legacy and the scandal which followed the opening of the Caillebotte room in 1897. He was also one of those who subscribed to buy Manet's *Olympia* – the first work by this artist to enter the French national collections (see p. 76). (see p. 76) GL

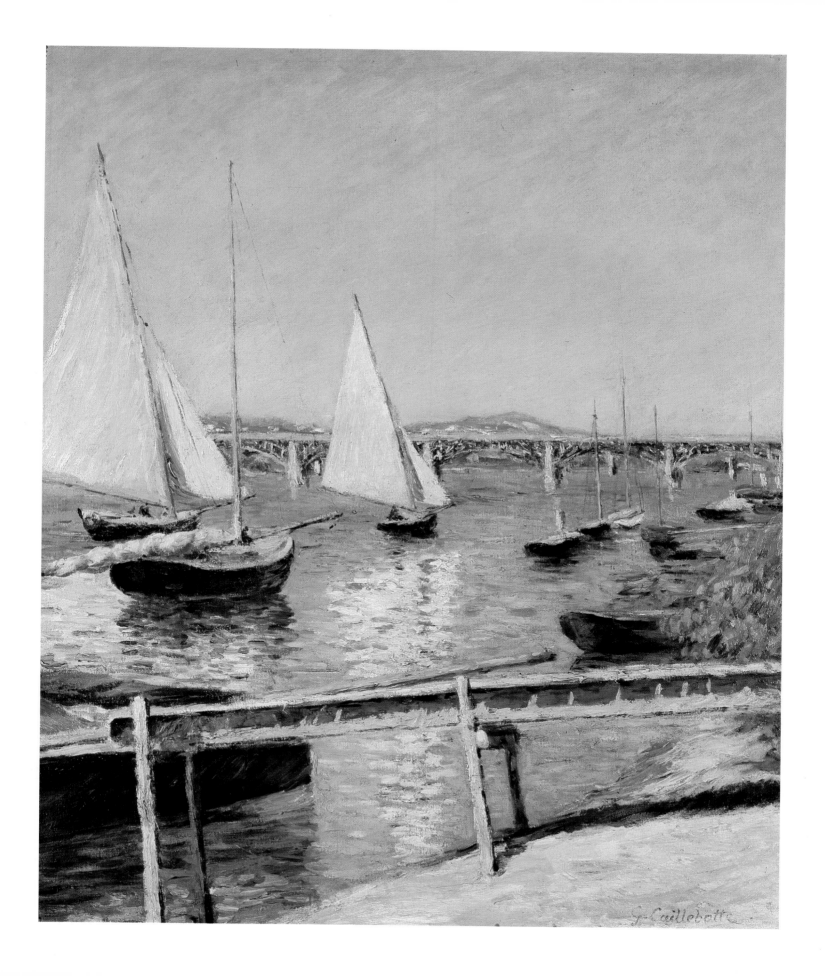

Mary CASSATT (1844–1926)

Femme cousant (*Woman Sewing*), c. 1880–82

Oil on canvas, $36\frac{1}{4} \times 24\frac{3}{4}$ (92×63)

Antonin Personnaz bequest, 1937 (R.F. 1937–20)

Like Eva Gonzalès and Berthe Morisot, who were pupils of Manet, Mary Cassatt was one of the special and unusual women connected with the Impressionist movement. Daughter of a rich Pittsburgh banker, she wanted to be a painter from a very early age. To achieve her ambition, she had to brave the scepticism and mockery of her family, at a time when it was not at all the thing for a woman to be an artist. Disappointed by the quality of the art instruction available in the United States, she soon returned to France where she had already spent part of her early childhood. After a short period in the studio of the Salon painter Chaplin, a good technician who specialized in society portraits, she turned resolutely to the study of the Old Masters, copying them with great enthusiasm during her travels in Italy, Spain, Belgium and Holland. She also tried her luck at the Paris Salon, where in 1874 Degas took special note of one of the portraits she had submitted: 'There is someone who thinks like me', he said to Joseph Tourny, a mutual friend.

Degas, for whom Cassatt had the greatest admiration, nevertheless waited three years before coming to visit her studio and inviting her to take part in the fourth Impressionist exhibition of 1879 – which she did, with *La loge* (*The Theatre Box*) and *La tasse de thé* (*The Cup of Tea*). She also showed in the fifth (1880), sixth (1881), and last Impressionist exhibitions (1886). One of the works she showed was the *Femme cousant*, reproduced here, which then became part of the famous collection left to the Louvre by Antonin Personnaz.

Though several of Cassatt's paintings are close to Manet (*Jeune femme en noir* [*Young Woman in Black*], 1833) and to Renoir (*A l'Opéra* [*At the Opera*], 1880), her work as a whole shows that she never swerved from her admiration for Japanese art. This is evident above all in the important series of prints which Cassatt showed so proudly at her first solo exhibition, held at Durand-Ruel's gallery in 1891. Moreover, she confines herself almost entirely to images of women and children, and achieves powerful effects within an intimist framework, as evinced by *Femme cousant*, which also demonstrates her exceptional talent as a colourist. It should not be forgotten that, by encouraging Durand-Ruel to show the Impressionists in the United States, and by becoming the enlightened adviser of the great American collector H. O. Havemeyer, Cassatt played a major role in the diffusion of Impressionism on the other side of the Atlantic.   CF-T

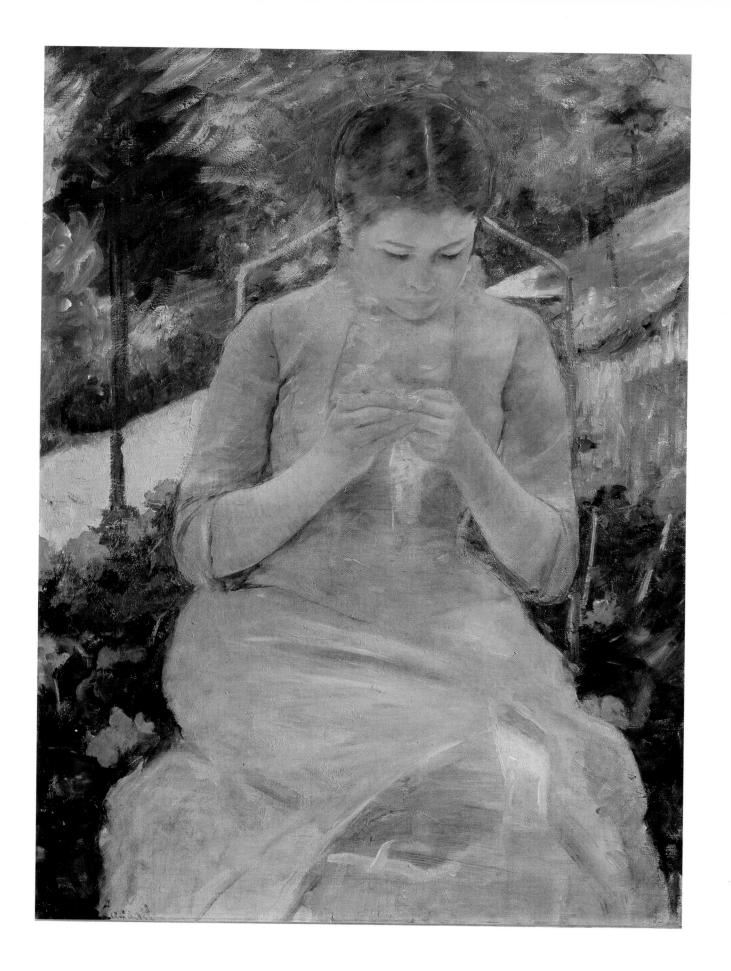

Paul CÉZANNE (1839–1906)

Une moderne Olympia (*A Modern Olympia*), c. 1873–74

Oil on canvas, $18\frac{1}{8} \times 21\frac{5}{8}$ (46 × 55)

Gift of Paul Gachet, 1951 (R.F. 1951–31)

Cézanne's earliest paintings, which were in dark tones, were strongly influenced by the Old Masters and by Delacroix, Daumier and Courbet. A typical painting of this period was an earlier one also entitled *Une moderne Olympia* (1870, formerly in the Pellerin Collection), painted in response to Manet's large canvas which had provoked such a scandal in the Salon of 1865 (see p. 76).

A few years later, Cézanne tackled the theme again, but this second version is quite different. Its brilliant, sparkling hues and dashing execution recall the paintings of Fragonard. Cézanne's style was at this point evolving towards Impressionism. It was during a visit to Auvers-sur-Oise as the guest of Dr Gachet, who later owned the painting, that the artist, inspired by an animated discussion about painting, picked up his brush to create this colourful sketch. In it he makes a new and more audacious interpretation of the subject. The contrast between the nudity of the woman, who is unveiled by a negress, and the elegant dress of the man in black, seated on a sofa with his back to us and looking at her, along with the strange little dog in the foreground, helps to give the scene an erotic, theatrical atmosphere which is accentuated by the presence of the curtain on the left. The bearded figure is strangely like Cézanne himself.

At the first Impressionist exhibition of 1874 this hallucinatory vision conjured up by Cézanne attracted the mockery of both public and critics. One critic saw it as 'a fantastic figure appearing to an opium-smoker in an opium-laden sky. This naked, rosy apparition, driven on by a kind of demon in the cloudy empyrean, in which is hatched this fragment of an artificial paradise, like a vision of voluptuous pleasure, has stifled even the bravest . . . and M. Cézanne seems no more than a kind of madman, with the fit on him, painting the fantasies of *delirium tremens*.' (Marc de Montifaud, *L'Artiste*, 1 May 1874.)   SG-P

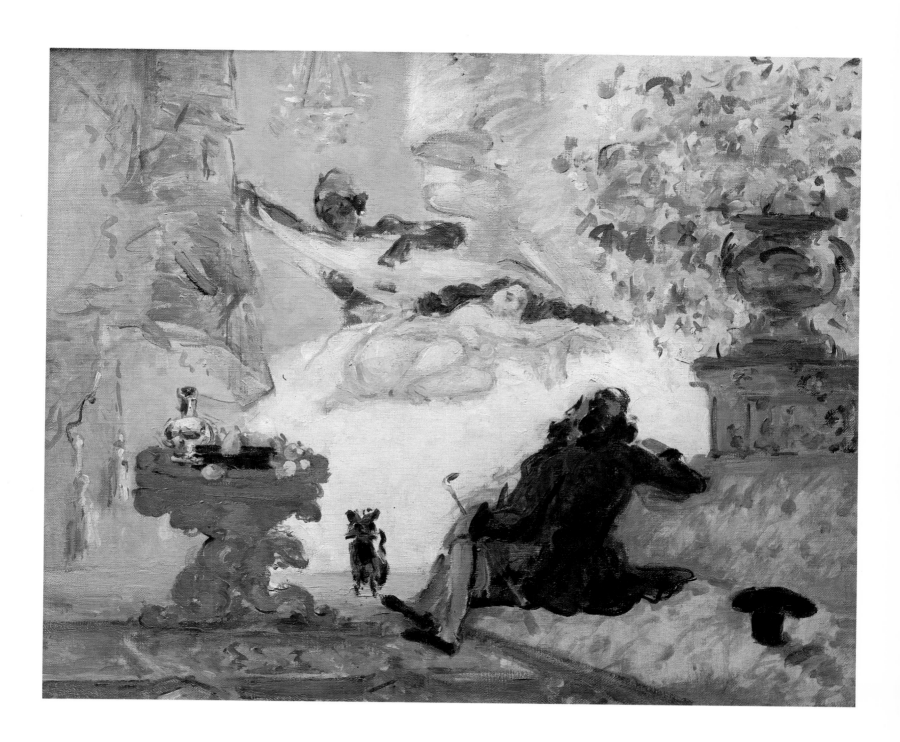

Paul CÉZANNE (1839–1906)

La maison du pendu, Auvers-sur-Oise

(*The House of the Hanged Man, Auvers-sur-Oise*), 1873

Oil on canvas, $21\frac{5}{8} \times 26$ (55×66)

Count Isaac de Camondo bequest, 1911 (R.F. 1970)

La maison du pendu, like *Une moderne Olympia* (see p. 24), was among the works by Cézanne shown at the first Impressionist exhibition of 1874, and it was just as badly received: 'when it comes to landscape, M. Cézanne sees fit not to take us right up to his *Maison du pendu* . . . he makes us stop half way there.' (Marc de Montifaud, *L'Artiste*, 1 May 1874.)

This canvas, painted at Auvers-sur-Oise, shows Cézanne under the influence of his older mentor, Pissarro, who was then living at Pontoise. Although Cézanne here was still using a thick impasto and continued to employ the palette-knife in places, he was at this time abandoning dark tonalities in order to substitute brighter hues, while at the same time adopting the broken Impressionist touch. He remained faithful to his objective of constructing space rigorously, something which he for his part communicated to Pissarro. It is interesting to compare this village landscape with contemporary works by Pissarro (see p. 114), in order to study the influence the two painters exercised on one another at this period, when they were working together.

As well as showing a change of technique, this painting bears witness to a new choice of subject-matter. Henceforward Cézanne was to abandon dramatic and literary themes in favour of insignificant subjects like this cross-roads. The subject has become a mere pretext; it is now only the 'motif', and is given its full meaning through the artist's interpretation.

This painting is one of the few signed by the artist (in red, in the bottom left-hand corner). As for the title – it does not in fact (as the art-historian Venturi points out) derive from an actual tragic event. Can we surmise, then, that this is a last vestige of the romanticism of Cézanne's earlier period?

This painting, the fruit of Cézanne's own revision and transformation of Impressionism, which he thereby turned into an entirely personal creation, represented the artist in the Centennial Exhibition of French Art held at the International Exhibition of 1889.   SG-P

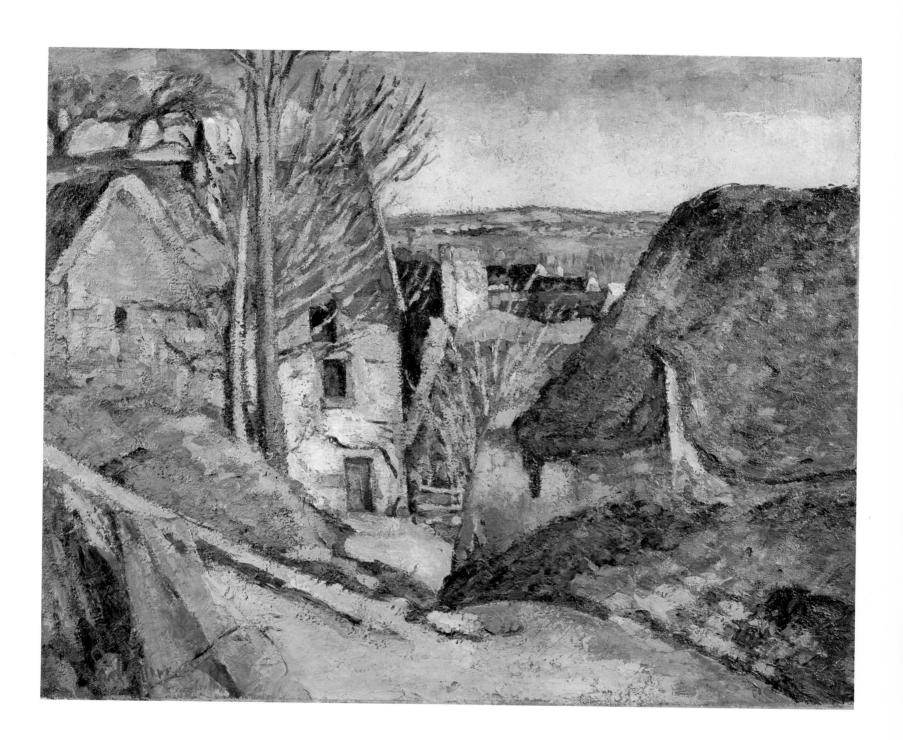

Paul CÉZANNE (1839–1906)

L'Estaque: vue du golfe de Marseille

(L'Estaque: View of the Bay of Marseilles), c. 1878–79

Oil on canvas, $23\frac{1}{4} \times 28\frac{3}{4}$ (59 × 73)

Gustave Caillebotte bequest, 1894 (R.F. 2761)

Cézanne's mother owned a house at L'Estaque, west of Marseilles, where the artist took refuge during the Franco-Prussian war of 1870–71. He afterwards returned several times, drawn no doubt by the Mediterranean, since his few seascapes were all painted there.

In 1876 Cézanne described to Pissarro the panoramic landscape which stretched before him: 'your letter finds me at the seaside, at L'Estaque. I've begun work on two little paintings which show the sea . . . It's like a playing-card. Red roofs against the blue sea . . . there are themes here which would encourage one to spend three or four months' work on them . . . since the vegetation doesn't alter. The olive-trees and pines keep all their foliage. The sun is so brilliant that it seems as if objects rise up in silhouette, not merely in black and white, but in blue and red and brown and violet . . . it's the antithesis of modelling.'

This view, looking down into the Bay of Marseilles, which was probably painted two or three years later, also has the appearance of a playing-card, in the way that the planes of colour are flat and well delineated. A similar effect had been achieved by Manet in his *Le fifre* of 1886 (p. 78), which was severely criticized by contemporary critics for this very reason. The composition of this painting of L'Estaque is divided into four distinct zones, each marked by their different treatment and colour. In the foreground is the shoreline, the heaviest and most thickly painted part; then the smooth blue surface of the water interrupted here and there by the white fleck of a sail; and then the range of mountains with a thin strip of sky above. The horizon is placed extremely high. The synthesis of planes, which seem to rear up towards the spectator as they get further away, constitutes an abolition of traditional perspective which seems to go beyond the boundaries of Impressionism.

Another, rather different version of this view, entitled *La mer à L'Estaque (The Sea at L'Estaque)*, in which the tall factory chimney also appears, entered the Louvre as part of the Picasso Collection.

SG-P

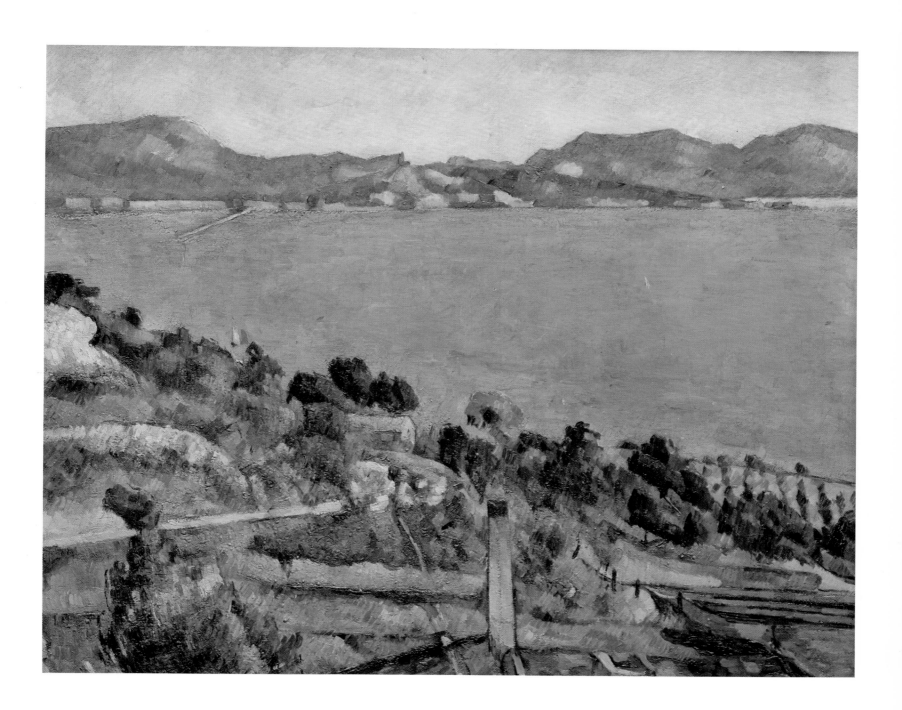

Paul CÉZANNE (1839–1906)

Le vase bleu *(The Blue Vase)*, c. 1885–87

Oil on canvas, 24 × 19⅝ (61 × 50)

Count Isaac de Camondo bequest, 1911 (R.F. 1973)

Cézanne is here more interested in colour modulation than in the depiction of flowers in bloom. Once again the subject is put at the service of one of his major preoccupations: the way light falls on objects and the resultant changes of colour. Space is constructed by means of a skilful play of verticals and horizontals and of a balanced distribution of volumes, while the harmony of the whole is ensured by the subtle use of different blues. The composition is centred exactly on the vase standing on the table.

Ten years earlier, at Auvers-sur-Oise, Cézanne had painted a number of flower pieces (of which the Jeu de Paume has several examples, thanks in the main to the gift made by Dr Gachet's son), but here he adds a new element: apples. Prominent because of their colour, they recall his still-lifes with fruit, which are much more numerous than the flower paintings. Cézanne once said to Gachet that he'd 'given up flowers. They fade immediately. Fruit is more reliable.' This canvas is enriched by the association of the two themes that had once led to Cézanne's being nicknamed 'Flowers and Fruit'. The apparent simplicity and sobriety of this painting are far removed from the exuberance and richness of Renoir's flower-pieces. It is interesting to recall that this painting first belonged to Vollard, the famous picture-dealer, who also represented Renoir, Gauguin and Picasso.

Le vase bleu was shown at the Cézanne retrospective organized as part of the Salon d'Automne of 1904, two years before the artist's death. SG-P

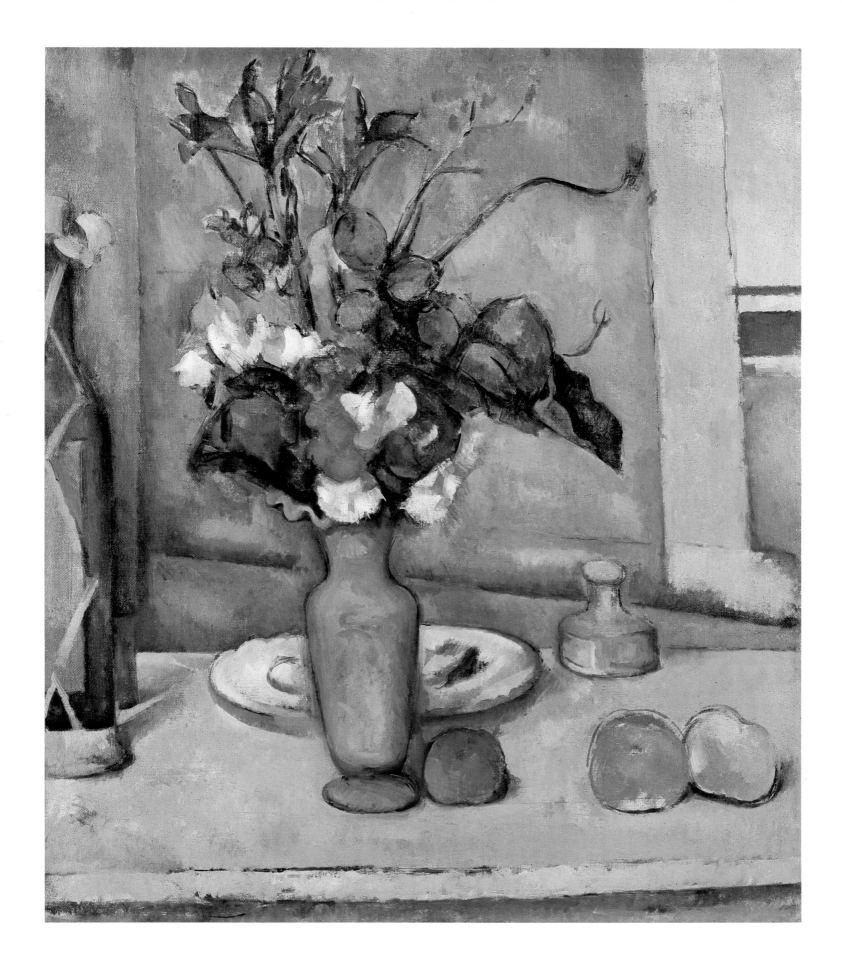

Paul CÉZANNE (1839–1906)

La femme à la cafetière (*Woman with a Coffee-pot*), c. 1890–95

Oil on canvas, $51\frac{1}{8} \times 37\frac{3}{4}$ (130 × 96)

Gift of M. and Mme Jean-Victor Pellerin, 1956 (R.F. 1956–31)

'The culmination of art is figure painting', Cézanne once said to Vollard. The artist painted portraits chiefly at the beginning and end of his career. He has been criticized for the abstracted air of his figures, who are sometimes compared to the enigmatic personages of Piero della Francesca. Cézanne tried to render, not fugitive expressions animating a face, but the essence of the model, his or her character; and hence produced these imposing effigies whose stability and monumentality remind one of Zurbarán. This is the impression one gets from *La femme à la cafetière*. Extreme slowness of execution and a certain shyness explain why Cézanne took his models from among those closest to him (above all his wife), and from among friends and the people he came across at the Jas de Bouffan (for example, farm-workers and servants, see also p. 34). This woman, with her hieratic pose, must be one such, though she cannot be identified with certainty.

Portraits such as this one prove how, in Cézanne's work, the exploration of the plasticity of the forms, here very much simplified, takes precedence over psychological analysis. The woman's body, a heavy sculptural mass, is studied as if it were still-life – in fact, the artist demanded of his models the same immobility that he got from apples. The woman's arms, following the example set by the coffee-pot and the cup, obey Cézanne's recommendation that 'nature should be rendered as a sphere, a cylinder or a cone'. This geometricization of volumes, together with the perspective used for the table, whose surface is tilted up, is the precursor of Cubism. (See also *Les joueurs de cartes*, p. 34, and *Nature morte aux oignons*, p. 38.)

This rigorously constructed work is a good illustration of the famous statement attributed to Cézanne, that 'drawing and colour are not separate; one draws as one paints; the more harmonious the colour, the more precise the draughtsmanship. When the colour reaches full richness, form reaches full plenitude. The secret of drawing and modelling lies in contrasts and juxtapositions of tone.'

SG-P

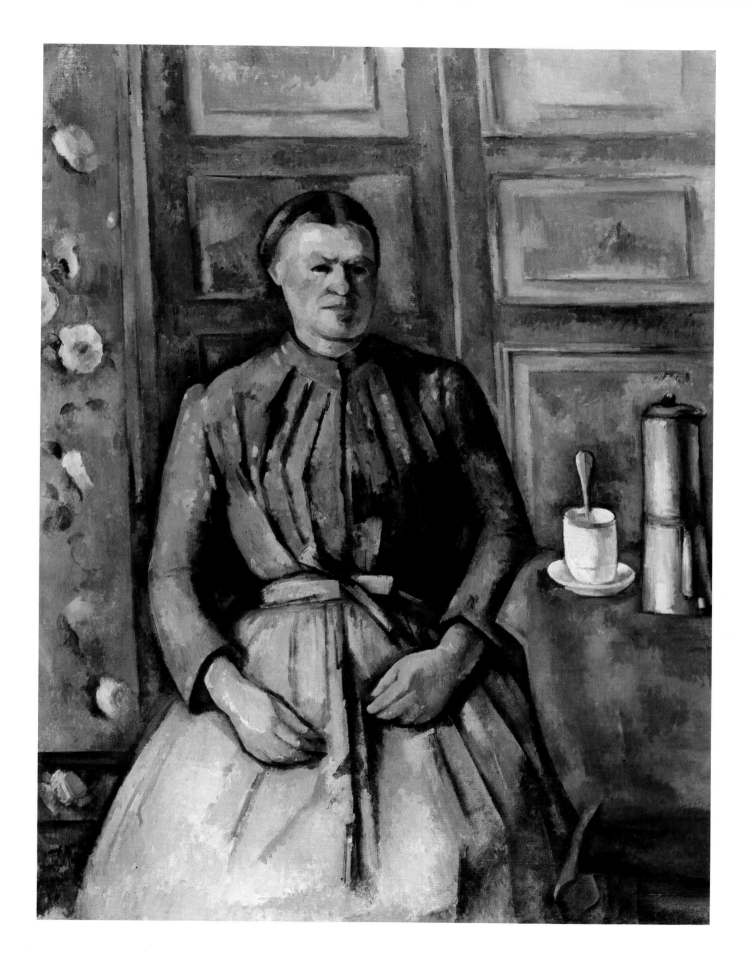

Paul CÉZANNE (1839–1906)

Les joueurs de cartes (The Card-players), c. 1890–95

Oil on canvas, $18\frac{1}{2} \times 18\frac{1}{2}$ (47 × 47)

Count Isaac de Camondo bequest, 1911 (R.F. 1969)

Cézanne is certain to have seen, in the museum at Aix-en-Provence, a painting of card-players which came from the studio of the Le Nain brothers. In the 1890s, he made use of this Caravaggesque theme on several occasions, but transformed it to accord with his own personal vision. For him everything was a pretext for the sophisticated exploration of line and volume. The central axis of this composition is the bottle catching the light; it divides the space into two symmetrical zones, and thereby accentuates the opposition of the players. They are ordinary country people and could well have been among those at his father's property at the Jas de Bouffan near Aix. The man smoking a pipe has been identified as 'Père Alexandre', the gardener there. (See also p. 32.)

Besides numerous preparatory studies, Cézanne devoted no less than five paintings to this theme. They differ in format, in the number of figures, and in the degree of importance given to the setting. The largest contains five figures (Merion, Barnes Foundation); another (New York, Metropolitan Museum) has four; while the three simplest have two apiece. Several theories have been put forward as to the order in which they were painted. The three simplified versions, of which this is one, seem to have been the subject of a long-pondered process of construction which leads one to believe that they are later than the two others, which are more cluttered but less elaborate. Faithful to his own temperament, Cézanne is here moving towards simplification, completely effacing the anecdotal aspect of this type of traditional genre-scene, and at the same time abandoning traditional perspective.

The recurrence of this theme in Cézanne's art during his last years has given rise to an interesting interpretation. Is the confrontation of the two players emblematic of the conflict between the artist and his father, as Cézanne tried to get the latter to give him recognition for his painting, which he here symbolizes by a playing-card?

SG-P

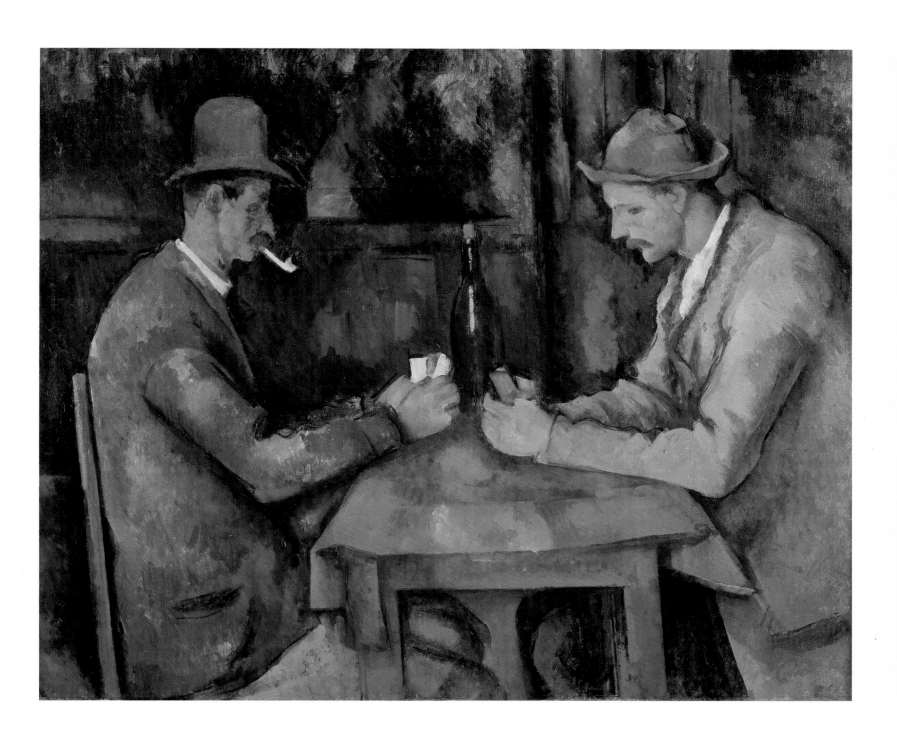

Paul CÉZANNE (1839–1906)

Baigneurs (*Bathers*), c. 1890–92

Oil on canvas, $23\frac{5}{8} \times 32\frac{1}{4}$ (60 × 82)

Gift of Baronne Eva Gebhard-Gourgaud, 1965 (R.F. 1965–3)

The airy space of *Baigneurs* creates a complete contrast to the enclosed one of *Les joueurs de cartes* (p. 34). Even the clouds take up the rhythm of the trees and the human bodies. The two subjects can be thought of as antithetical – the latter, portrayed in sombre hues, being associated with the notion of conflict, while the former, dominated by blues and greens, shows the artist trying to express the harmony of man and nature, and even a certain fusion between the two. Cézanne is perhaps thinking of his childhood at Aix, and of joyous bathes in the river Arc with his friends, Zola among them. He must also have seen soldiers bathing in this river.

The painter here analyses the integration of figure and landscape, following in the steps of masters such as Giorgione, Titian, Rubens and Poussin. His researches culminated in the creation of three large paintings of bathers, in which he revivified a theme already traditional in French art – Watteau, Boucher, Fragonard, Courbet and Renoir all painted women bathing. The theme is evident in Cézanne's work from 1870 onwards, and obsessed him particularly in his last years. He returned tirelessly in many of his paintings and watercolours to poses suggested by Old Master drawings and ancient sculptures.

In this example, one of the most complete and best constructed, the figures are used to make a balanced pyramidal composition, like a tympanum, a device frequently used in Italian art. Like the bottle in *Les joueurs de cartes*, the central tree serves as the axis. The man holding the piece of drapery seems to have been inspired by a Signorelli drawing and has also been compared (by Charles Sterling) to a figure in El Greco's *Laocoön*. In other variants, the bathers are arranged to make a frieze.

This painting was shown at the Salon d'Automne of 1904, and had an important influence on the young painters of the time. Several of them owned versions of it, among them Degas, Matisse and Picasso.   SG-P

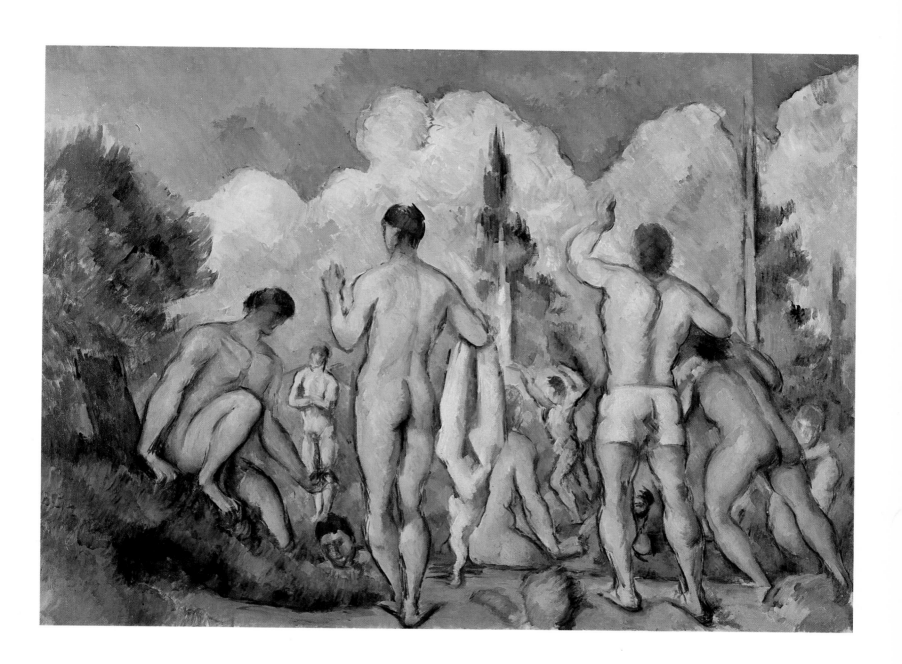

Paul CÉZANNE (1839–1906)

Nature morte aux oignons (*Still-life with Onions*), c. 1895

Oil on canvas, 30 × 32¼ (66 × 82)
Auguste Pellerin bequest, 1929 (R.F. 2817)

The medium of still-life, which was in harmony both with Cézanne's character and with his method of working, retained his attention throughout his career. Following the example of the Spanish and Dutch masters, who were attuned to the 'silent life of objects', Cézanne was attracted by the poetry of the familiar accessories of daily life. But it is the name of Chardin which suggests itself even more forcefully in his work than those of Vermeer, Zurbarán or Goya; and Cézanne doubtless saw and admired the paintings by Chardin which became part of the Louvre collection in 1869, as a result of the Lacaze gift. In order to give the illusion of depth, for example, Cézanne borrows from Chardin the device of a knife placed diagonally in the composition – something that Manet had also made use of.

In addition to fruit, whose spherical forms, like those of onions, were an ideal subject for his investigations into the nature of volume, Cézanne here represents a number of other simple objects, some of which can still be seen today in his studio at Aix-en-Provence (such as pottery and pieces of glass). This fidelity to the same props shows that the painter concentrated his attention on the disposition of the objects and on the architecture of the composition, and also studied the fall of light on the forms. 'Yes, draw', he wrote in 1905; 'but it is reflections that wrap things round – light, which by its general reflection, provides them with an envelope'.

On this table with its scalloped edge, Cézanne introduces, as in many of the still-lifes of his last period, a decorative piece of drapery which counterbalances the vertical made by the bottle and conceals the rigorously ordered construction of the picture. This drapery stands out, like the bottle, against a totally empty neutral background which differentiates this painting from other late still-lifes which are much more crowded. Cézanne at this time was adopting a new perspective system which was to open the door to Cubism: the objects are seen from above, and from several different viewpoints at once. SG-P

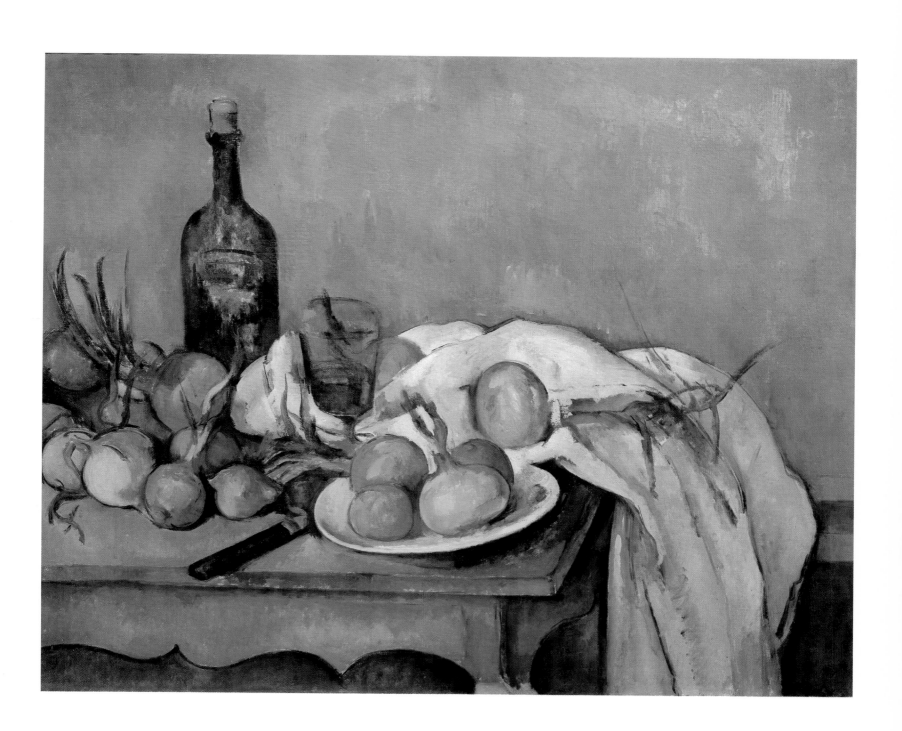

Edgar DEGAS (1834–1917)

La famille Bellelli (*The Bellelli Family*), 1858–60

Oil on canvas, 78¾ × 98⅜ (200 × 250)

Purchased in 1918 (R.F. 2210)

When Degas died, this family portrait was one of the many paintings found in his studio. It is an early work, until then practically unknown, representing Degas' aunt, Laure Bellelli (née de Gas), her husband Gennaro Bellelli, and their two daughters Giovanna and Giulia. Preceded by numerous drawings and sketches, the canvas was begun in 1858 in Florence where Degas stayed for a long period during one of his journeys to Italy and where Bellelli, a supporter of Cavour and in exile from Naples, was also living at the time.

Degas was twenty-five when he began the painting, and its mastery is astonishing even now. It is not merely that the young artist had so completely assimilated the lessons of the painters he admired – Van Dyck and the Florentine Bronzino among the Old Masters, and Ingres among the moderns – but also that he embues this work with a new spirit through his sensitive representation of contemporary reality. The way the people are dressed, the furniture, the mirrors (providing additional images), the hangings, objects like the work-basket on the table – all these immediately place the people in their own epoch and in the bourgeois milieu to which they belong.

At the same time few portraits so clearly reveal the psychology of their models: Laure Bellelli, a little haughty, neurasthenic, and estranged from a husband who here appears eclipsed and distant; the little girls, Giovanna standing under her mother's protective arm, Giulia seated half off the chair – the only one who seems to want to break the constraints. Using a device which appears frequently in his work, Degas introduces an additional allusion by showing, in a drawing hanging behind Laure Bellelli, a portrait of her grandfather, Hilaire-René de Gas, who had recently died – which explains why the sitters are dressed in mourning.   AD

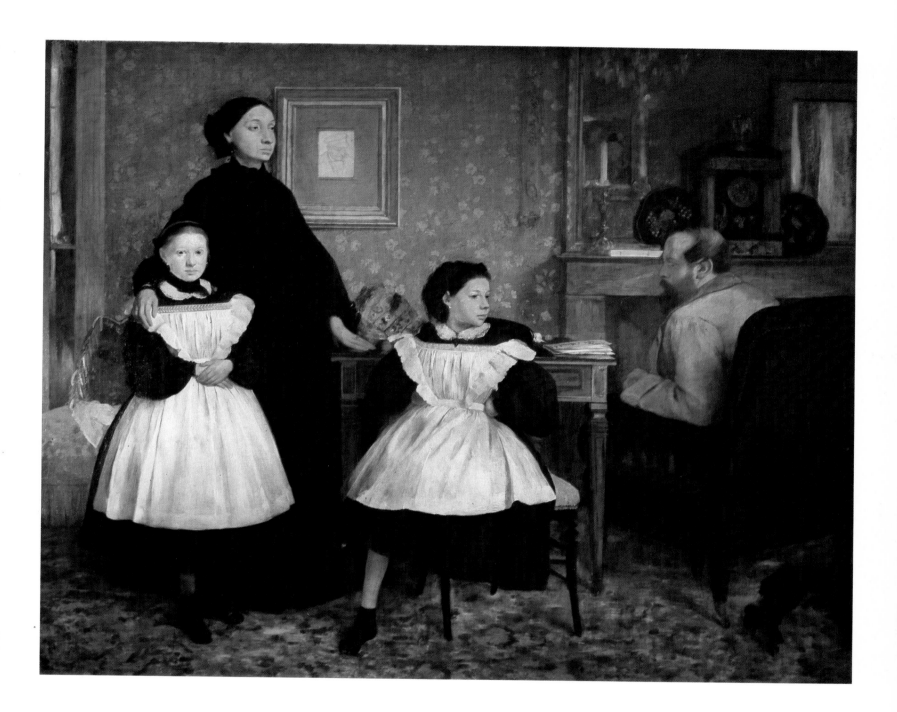

Edgar DEGAS (1834–1917)

L'orchestre de l'Opéra (*The Orchestra of the Opéra*), *c.* 1868–69

Oil on canvas, $22\frac{1}{4} \times 18\frac{1}{8}$ (56·5 × 46)

Purchased from Mlle Marie Dihau, but retained by her for her lifetime, 1924; entered the Louvre in 1935 (R.F. 2417)

Since it entered the Jeu de Paume collection, this painting has been entitled *Musicians in an Orchestra*, because it portrays several of Degas' friends as violinists – a painter, a medical student, the ballet-master of the Opéra – who were indeed not violinists at all. But in our opinion it should once again be known by the title the artist gave it. His idea was, as he wrote in one of his notebooks, to create, in a highly naturalistic style, 'a series on instruments and instrumentalists and on their forms – the way the violinist twists his arms, his hands and his neck; the way the cheeks of the bassoonists and oboe-players swell up and deflate, etc.'

Being himself musical and enjoying French and Italian music in particular, Degas delighted in the company of musicians, of whom he made numerous portraits. In 1868 he became friendly with Désiré Dihau, a bassoonist at the Opéra, and also with his sister Marie, who was a singer, and through them became acquainted with other members of the orchestra who used to meet at a restaurant near the opera house called 'Chez la Mère Lefebvre', on the Rue de la Tour d'Auvergne. When Dihau asked Degas to paint his portrait, Degas first thought of representing him on his own, but then hit on the idea of this group painting, where – for the first time – the emphasis is put on the musicians who generally pass unnoticed at a performance. In the box nearest the stage, high up to the right, can be seen the face of the composer Emmanuel Chabrier; in the orchestra pit, all the musicians are portraits of identifiable people. Turned towards a conductor who remains invisible to the right, they are: Pillet (cello); Désiré Dihau (bassoon); Altès (flute); Lancien and Gout (first violins); and Gouffé (double-bass). The scroll of Gouffé's instrument is silhouetted against the stage where, in the dazzling artificial light, several ballerinas in pink and blue tutus dance, their heads and feet cropped – a daring evocation of the performance as it would have appeared in reality. The composition, designed with great sophistication, is a play of oblique lines made by the instruments and the legs of the dancers against the strong horizontals of the footlights and the edge of the orchestra pit, with an unexpected set of rectangles created by the back of Gouffé's chair and the wall of the auditorium next to the box. GL

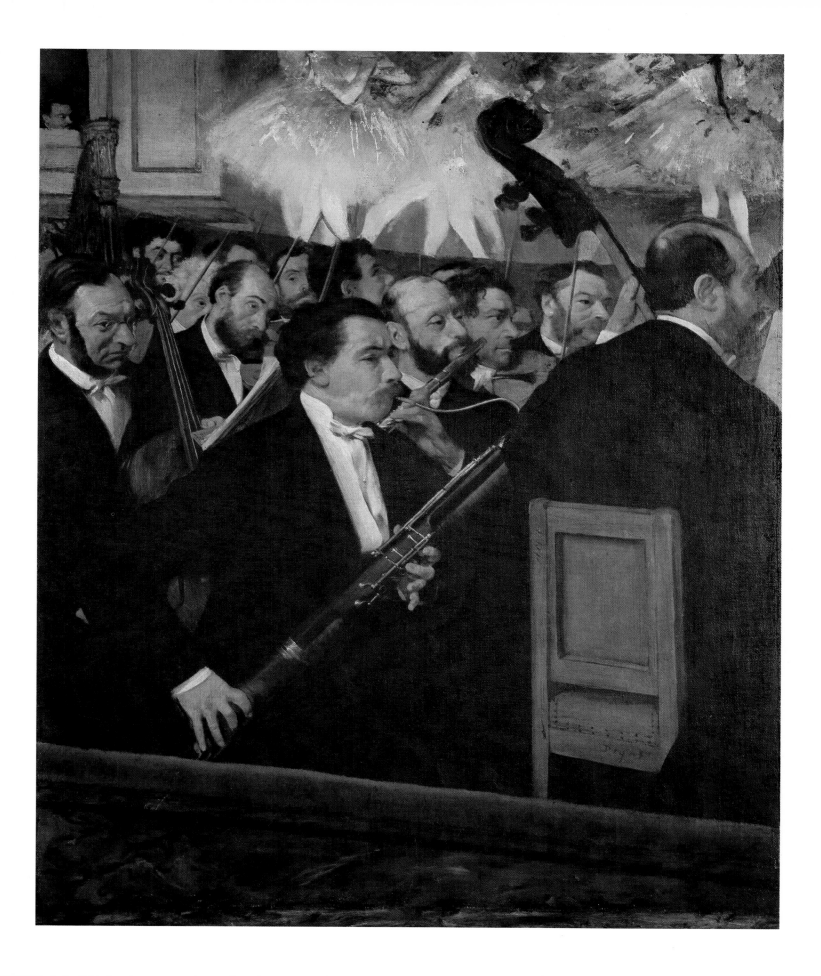

Edgar DEGAS (1834–1917)

La classe de danse (*The Dancing class*, originally entitled *Preliminary Steps*), c. 1873–75

Oil on canvas, $33\frac{1}{2} \times 29\frac{1}{2}$ (85 × 75)

Count Isaac de Camondo bequest, 1911 (B.F. 1976)

In 1872 Degas began work on a series depicting the life of ballerinas, as he observed them at the Paris Opéra in the Rue Le Peletier, often making several versions of the same subject. Paintings on this theme appeared in the Impressionist exhibitions of 1874, 1876 and 1877, but this one does not seem to have been among them. It was, however, the subject, as is shown by an X-ray, of numerous rehandlings which enable us to trace the creative processes of the artist. Although, in his *Journal* for 13 February 1974, Edmond de Goncourt spoke of Degas as 'the man who is at the present moment best able, in the copying of contemporary life, to catch its spirit', Degas in fact spent a long time on his compositions, first of all building up a huge repertory of gestures, figure by figure. Here all the alterations serve to emphasise the focus on the role of the ballet-master Jules Perrot in the composition. He was at first turned towards the back wall but the final pose is given in a quick study in thinned oil colour on paper dated 1875 (Philadelphia, Henry McIlhenny Collection), which indicates that the painting itself was thus altered in that year. Two dancers in the foreground at first looked towards the viewer. One, wearing a tutu with a green ribbon, has her back to us, while the other is obscured – one sees only part of her face – behind the new figure of the dancer seated on the piano and scratching her back. This casual pose was noted by a reviewer writing for an English newspaper, *The Echo*, on 22 April 1876, when the painting was shown at the Deschamps Gallery in London. There it was soon sold to a collector, Captain Henry Hill of Brighton, who showed it, together with *L'absinthe*, in a local exhibition in the autumn of 1876. Sold at Christie's in May 1889, the painting returned to France by way of Theo van Gogh, who was then working for the picture-dealer Goupil. GL

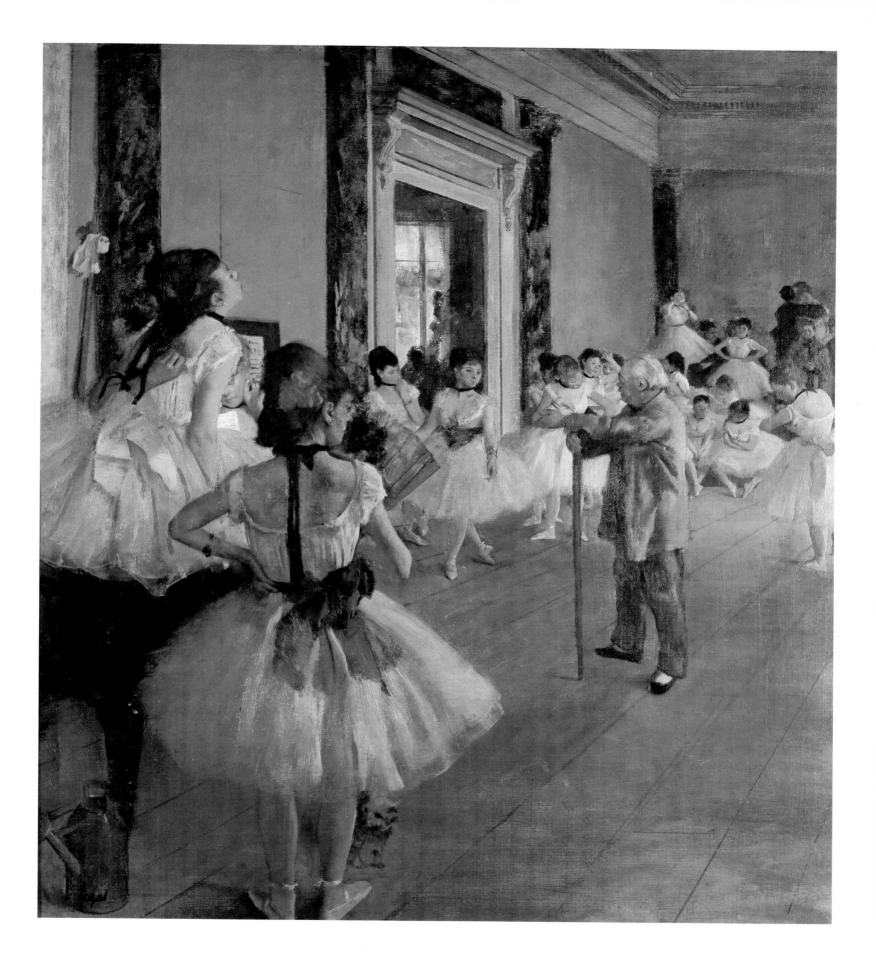

Edgar DEGAS (1834–1917)

L'absinthe, 1876

Oil on canvas, $36\frac{1}{4} \times 26\frac{3}{4}$ (92×68)

Count Isaac de Camondo bequest, 1911 (R.F. 1984)

Degas here reinterprets, in more than one respect, the traditional Flemish theme of drinkers in a tavern. He presents a resolutely contemporary scene, a sort of illustration to Zola's novel *L'Assommoir* (*The Dram-shop*), which was appearing in parts that same year. Two figures sit silently before their glasses, apparently ignoring one another, on a bench at the Nouvelle Athènes café in the Place Pigalle in Paris, which was the latest haunt of Manet, Degas and their friends. A year or so earlier they had abandoned the famous Café Guerbois and were drawn to the Nouvelle Athènes by the personality of the painter and print-maker Marcellin Desboutin. It is Desboutin whom Degas represents here, wearing the same bohemian costume which is to be seen in the full-length portrait of him by Manet, done in 1875 (*L'artiste*, Museu de Arte de São Paulo), which was rejected by the Salon of 1876. In Degas' painting, a supporting role is played by the pantomime actress Ellen Andrée, who also posed for Renoir, Manet and Gervex. Dazed, she sits beside Desboutin, in front of a glass of absinthe, with its sulphurous bright green colouring.

Degas' originality, in this masterly composition which demonstrates both direct observation and psychological acuity, is to have placed the figures in the upper right-hand corner. The rest of the picture – seen as if the artist was sitting at a neighbouring table – is filled with empty table-tops on which have been thrown some newspapers mounted on wooden rods. These were provided for customers who spent hours waiting, looking out at the passers-by, just as Desboutin is here looking in the direction of a window covered by a net curtain and reflected brightly in the mirror behind him. Characterized by a subtle understanding of Japanese art, this kind of composition was taken up again by Degas in his portrait of Duranty (Glasgow Museums and Art Galleries). It was Duranty who, in his book *La Nouvelle Peinture* (*The New Painting*), wrote, speaking of Degas, that 'the appearance of things and people can take on a thousand unexpected aspects when we meet them in reality'.

It was as a representative of this 'new painting' that Degas soon found a purchaser in England: Captain Henry Hill, a Brighton collector who in the autumn of 1876 showed the picture in a local exhibition (see also p. 44). The trivial subject-matter caused a scandal when the painting was shown again in 1893 at the Grafton Gallery in London, and it soon thereafter returned to France and – then entitled *L'apéritif* – became part of the Camondo Collection.   GL

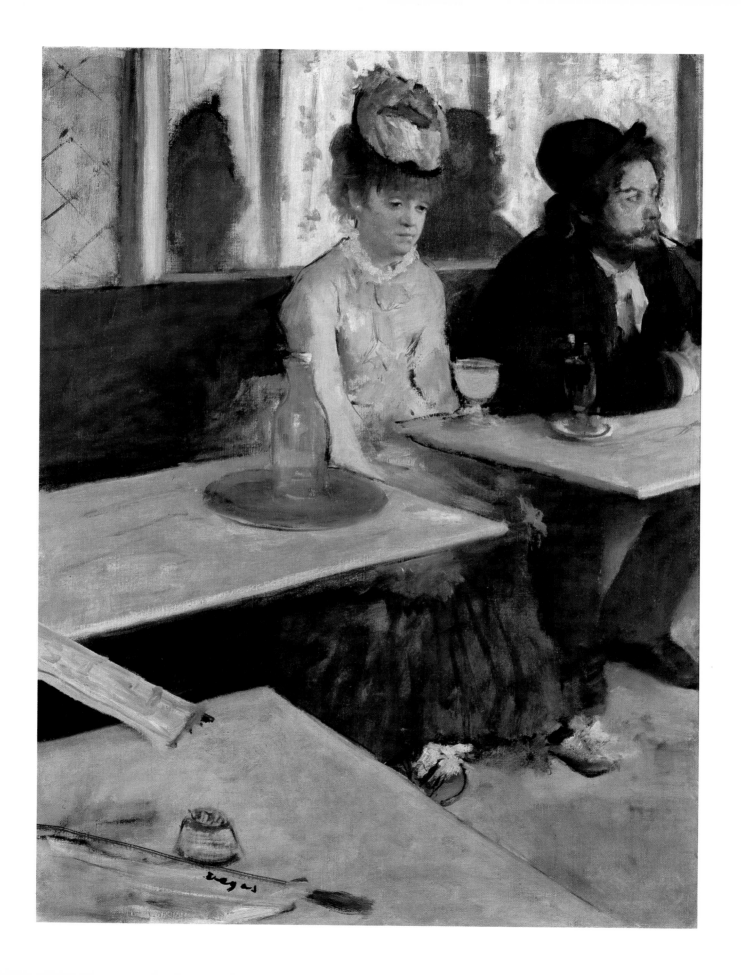

Edgar DEGAS (1834–1917)

L'étoile or La danseuse sur la scène

(*The Star* or *Dancer on Stage*), 1878

Pastel on paper, $23\frac{5}{8} \times 17\frac{3}{8}$ (60 × 44)

Gustave Caillebotte bequest, 1894, on deposit from the Department of Drawings at the Louvre (R.F. 12.258)

For about ten years Degas had concentrated on showing dancers at work – in rehearsal, resting, fatigued, even totally worn out – in the wings or in the rehearsal-rooms of the Opéra. But this suffering and effort were rewarded by the grace of the ballerinas when they appeared on stage. To begin with, Degas showed views of the whole ensemble, then he fixed his attention, as he does here, upon a single soloist isolated on stage, transformed by the footlights into an incarnation of feminine grace, while the other performers appear only as silhouettes half-hidden in the wings. From the objective study of a particular milieu, he now moves to this analysis of movement, which was soon to be continued in a series of sculptures, among them the remarkable *Grande danseuse habillée* (*Large Clothed Dancer*) of 1881 (illustrated on the back cover).

In 1878 he was preoccupied above all with a new exploration of the physical media of the artist, using pastel for preference in order to render the vaporous quality of the dancer's costume. He contrasts areas which are delicately finished with others that are rapidly coloured in. These latter allow the impression printed in monotype, which was the first state of the composition and which supplies its actual structure, to remain visible. This was a frequent technique with Degas, and here gives a remarkable solidity to those parts which are simply sketched in, such as the backcloth. Some particularly brightly lit areas, such as the neck and leg of the dancer, are balanced against touches of black (the dancer's floating ribbon, and the man to her left, who is a stage manager or admirer appearing in the wings) and strikingly set off this almost supernatural image of the artificial life of the stage. GL

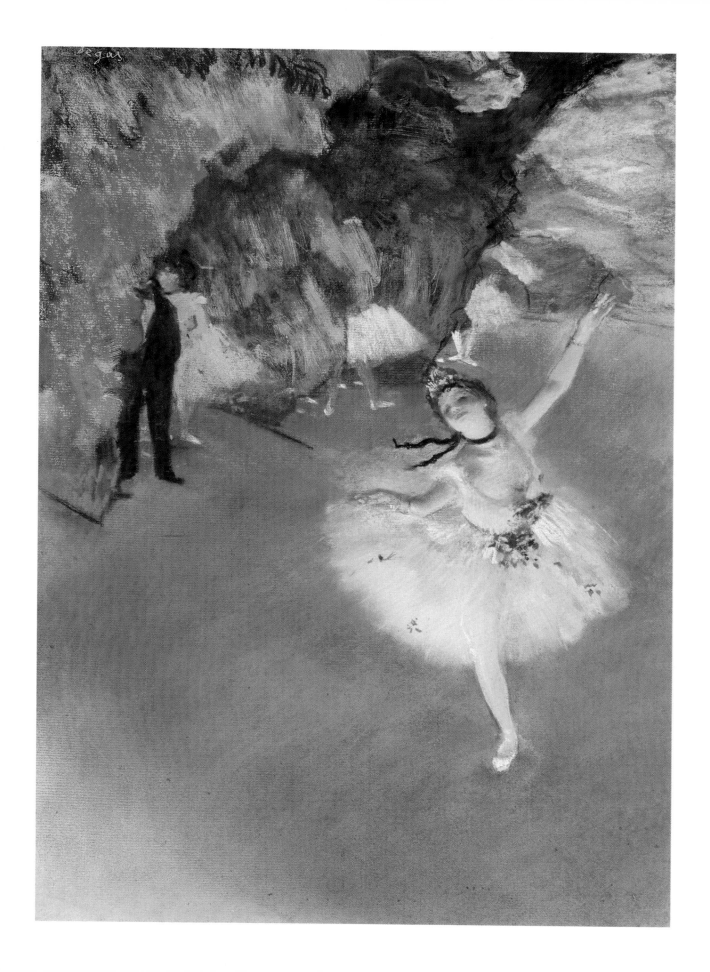

Edgar DEGAS (1834–1917)

Chevaux de courses devant les tribunes

(Racehorses in Front of the Stands), c. 1879

Thinned oil colour on canvas, $18\frac{1}{8} \times 24$ (46×61)

Count Isaac de Camondo bequest, 1911 (R.F. 1981)

From 1860 onwards, Degas began to be interested in horse-racing, an amusement he discovered in Normandy when visiting his friends the Valpinçons. It is sometimes difficult to date works on this theme, as it is one that he used frequently for twenty years. This example, painted in a thinned medium which gives a lighter and more transparent effect than conventional oils, is probably the painting listed as no. 63 in the fourth Impressionist exhibition of 1879 under the title *Chevaux de courses: essence (Racehorses: thinned oil colour)*. It was formerly thought that the picture was painted much earlier, before Degas' trip to New Orleans. The fact that several drawings, notably for one of the jockeys, date from around 1866 would appear to support this view.

Degas' paintings of horses are not only the results of single encounters with an especially interesting contemporary scene, whether a provincial entertainment or, as here, a Parisian one. They also grow from his study of paintings and drawings of the same subject-matter, by Géricault, Alfred de Dreux, and, as here, Meissonier. Meissonier's long-awaited painting of *Napoleon III à la bataille de Solférino* (Louvre), finally shown at the Salon of 1864, attracted copyists as soon as it entered the Musée du Luxembourg in August of that year. In his sketchbooks now in the Bibliothèque Nationale, Degas drew several riders from it, notably those seen from the rear in the left foreground, moving towards the group of the Emperor's general staff. The horses in the painting reproduced here, though now ridden by jockeys, are standing in very much the same way, but are differently placed; the one on the right in the original is put on the left, and vice-versa. Their movement away from one another accentuates the effect made by the open space of the race-track. There is a play of diagonals crossing one another which encompasses in addition the line of the stands and the barrier to the left, and also the long shadows cast by the horses. Despite the fact that he had borrowed his theme from another artist, Degas has here composed an original painting, alive and full of light, punctuated by the bright colours of the silks worn by the jockeys, with everything kept in balance by the horizontal band of the sky. The work no longer has anything in common with Meissonier's miniaturism.

It must also be remembered that, when Degas began his career, he was by no means hostile to the Salon as an institution, and took part in its exhibitions until the fall of the Second Empire.   GL

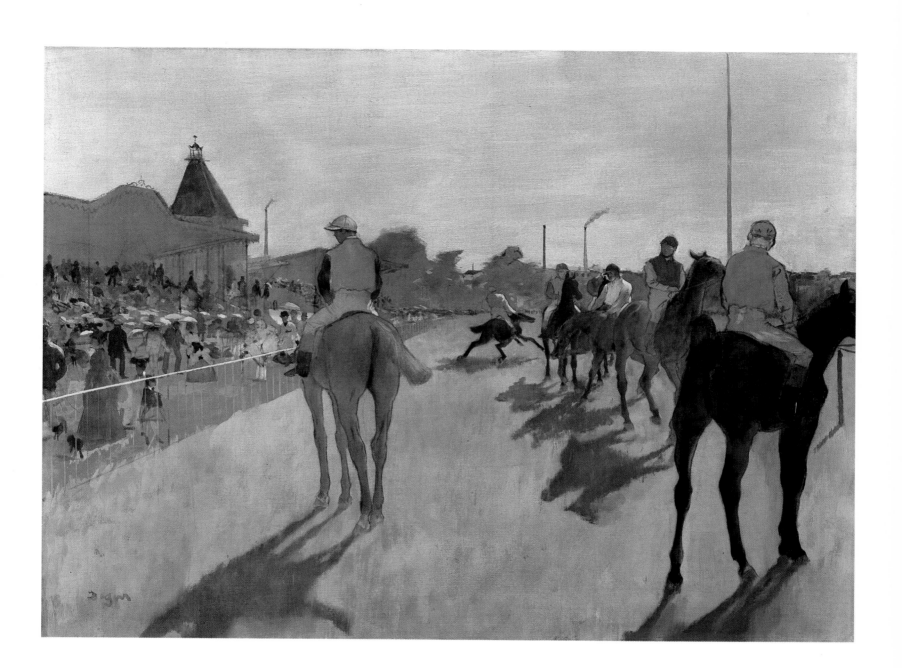

Edgar DEGAS (1834–1917)

Les repasseuses (*Women Ironing*), 1884

Oil on canvas, $29\frac{7}{8} \times 31\frac{7}{8}$ (76×81)

Count Isaac de Camondo bequest, 1911 (R.F. 1983)

After a visit to Degas, Edmond de Goncourt noted in his *Journal* on 13 February 1874: 'After many experiments, trial-runs and feelers put out in all directions, he has now fallen in love with the contemporary and, amidst the contemporary, has fixed his attentions on washerwomen and dancers. I cannot find fault with his choice, since I too, in *Manette Salomon*, lauded these two professions as those providing, in our time, the female models most suited to depiction by a contemporary painter.' The first of the *Repasseuses* by Degas is the pastel of 1869 acquired by the Louvre as part of the Personnaz bequest; it is the earliest study of a theme he took up many times in the course of perfecting it. The canvas illustrated here is one of the most famous examples. Painted in about 1884, it is a rehandling of a composition in pastel of two years earlier, now in the Durand-Ruel Collection, but contains a number of variations. These two women, hard at work and utterly exhausted, give us an uncompromising insight into the depth of human experience which Degas, born an aristocrat, had come to know, and which he also displays in *L'absinthe* (p. 46). These women ironing provide an echo of the naturalistic literature of the period – for example, Zola's *L'Assommoir* (*The Dram-shop*), published in 1877 – which inspired many artists, among them Steinlen and Forain. But this powerful image also demonstrates astonishing technical virtuosity, on a par with pastel in its rendering of texture. It must have made an impression on Picasso in 1904 during his Blue Period, when he adopted the theme and took it in the direction of pathos (New York, Solomon R. Guggenheim Museum).   CF-T

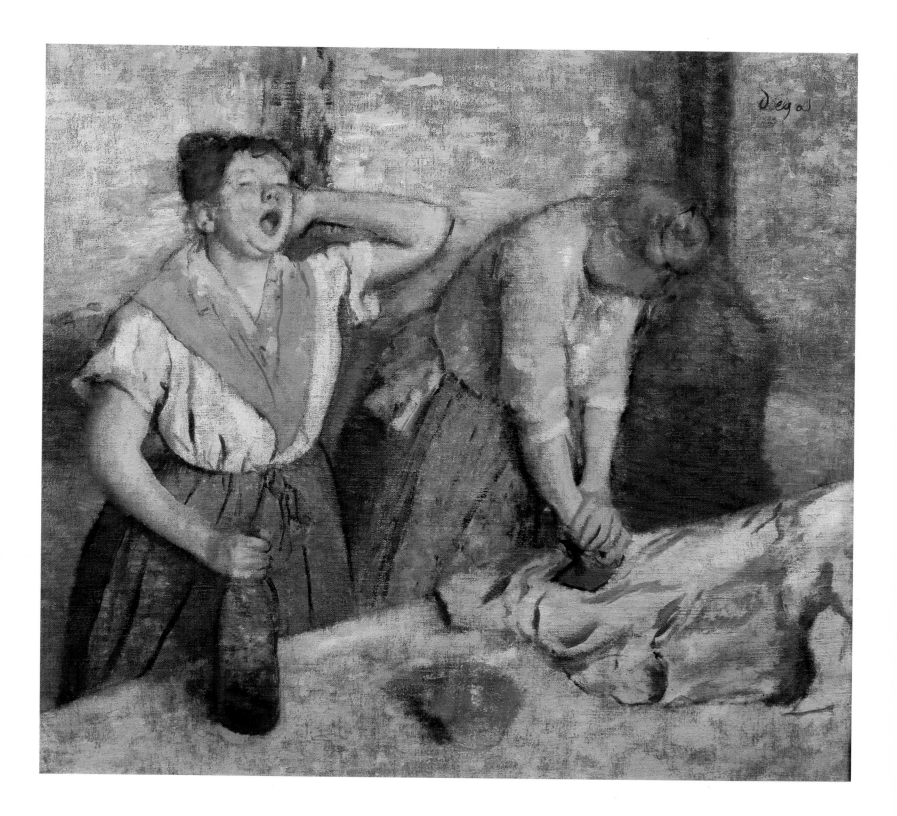

Edgar DEGAS (1834–1917)

Le tub (*The Tub*), 1886

Pastel on cardboard, $23\frac{5}{8} \times 32\frac{5}{8}$ (60 × 83)

Count Isaac de Camondo bequest, 1911; on deposit from the Department of Drawings in the Louvre

(R.F. 4046)

This famous painting by Degas entered the Louvre, along with *L'absinthe* and *Les repasseuses* (pp. 46, 52) as part of the magnificent Camondo bequest. The collection contained an important series of pastels by Degas showing women at their toilet. As the painter himself explained, this group of nudes, which occupied him intensely for a dozen or so years between about 1878 and 1890, was intended to represent 'the human animal pre-occupied with herself, like a cat licking itself'. 'Up till now,' he added, 'the nude has always been represented in poses which presuppose the presence of a spectator. But my women are simple, straightforward creatures interested only in what they are doing physically. Here's another, washing her feet – it's as if you were looking at her through the keyhole.' This candid parti-pris for unadorned observation, as opposed to the academic nudes which were always prized at the Salon – and which had only recently been attacked by Manet's *Olympia* (see p. 76) – shocked visitors to the final Impressionist exhibition of 1886, were Degas showed a series of his nudes.

At this time, the artist turned more and more frequently to pastel, carrying the technique to new and unequalled heights of virtuosity, often mixing distemper and thinned oil colour with it to get new effect of texture and light. Several years later, when his sight began to fail, he made sculpture the medium of his observations, taking up once again his favourite themes: dancers, horses and women at their toilet. In this pastel the originality of the spatial organization, where the plane of the still-life cuts boldly into the space occupied by the tub, owes much to Japanese art, from which painters were then borrowing new compositional formulae. Degas was a past-master at locking together different picture-planes. In this he influenced Gauguin at the beginning of his career, and also Bonnard, Vuillard and Maurice Denis who were to become the leaders of the Nabis. The continuing influence of Ingres (whose disciple Degas was) can be traced through Degas' nudes to the work of twentieth-century artists such as Maillol, Valadon and Picasso. CF-T

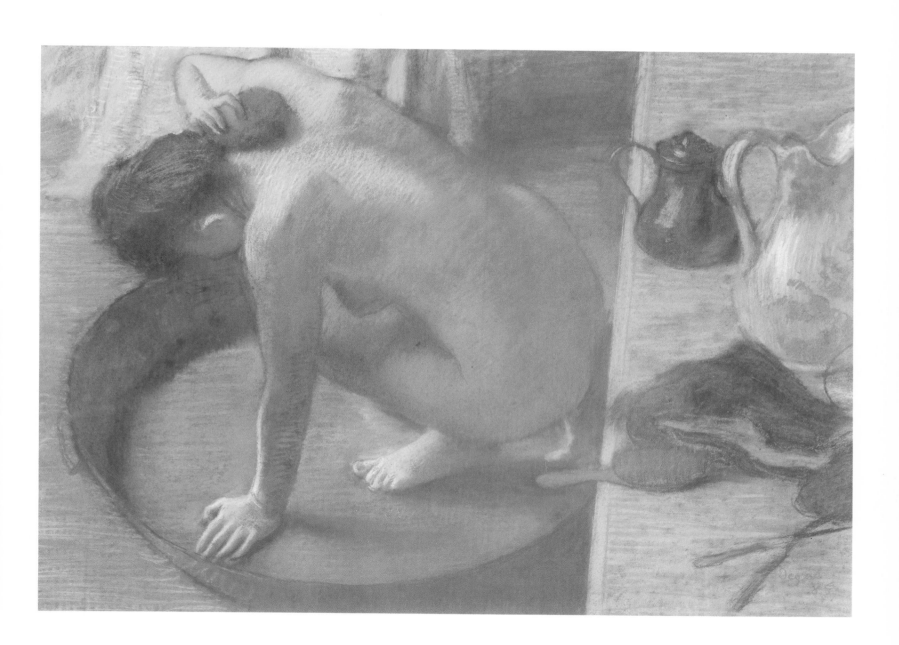

Paul GAUGUIN (1848–1903)

Les Alyscamps, Arles, 1888

Oil on canvas, $35\frac{7}{8} \times 28\frac{3}{8}$ (91×72)

Gift of Countess Vitali in memory of her brother, Viscount Guy du Cholet, 1923 (R.F. 1938–47)

'I went to Arles to join Vincent van Gogh, after numerous pleas from him. He said he wanted to set up a studio in the Midi, of which I was to be the head'. So wrote Gauguin in 'Diverses Choses' ('A Variety of Things'), a manuscript of 1896–97. These two ardent solitaries thus came together in the Midi in the autumn of 1888, Gauguin extremely conscious of his prestige as head of the Pont-Aven Group and Van Gogh avid for comfort and human warmth.

The view of the celebrated Christian necropolis of the Alyscamps, with the cupola of the Chapel of Saint-Honorat in the background, inspired the two artists to paint a group of paintings in which it is difficult to distinguish the influences each had on the other. Gauguin's brilliant version shows a 'synthetist' understanding of the landscape, which is boldly cut into zones of colour delimited by decorative arabesques which pay no attention to exact topography. Gauguin here employs particularly bright hues and brushwork that harks back to Impressionism in its fragmentation, to interpret the brilliance of the Mediterranean scene. But it is the arbitrariness of the colour that is so striking – for example, the blue tree-trunk and the violent red splash on the right. It shows clearly how Gauguin opened the way for modernism, from the Nabis to the abstractionists of the present day via the Fauves. This picture illustrates the lesson that Gauguin had just taught the young painter Sérusier, shortly before his own departure from Brittany: 'How do you see that tree? It's green? So use green, the most beautiful on your palette; and that shadow – rather blue, is it? Don't be afraid, paint it as blue as you can.' This conversation, recorded by Maurice Denis, gave rise to the famous picture by Sérusier known as *Le talisman*, and thus led to the formation of the group of artists known as the Nabis. CF-T

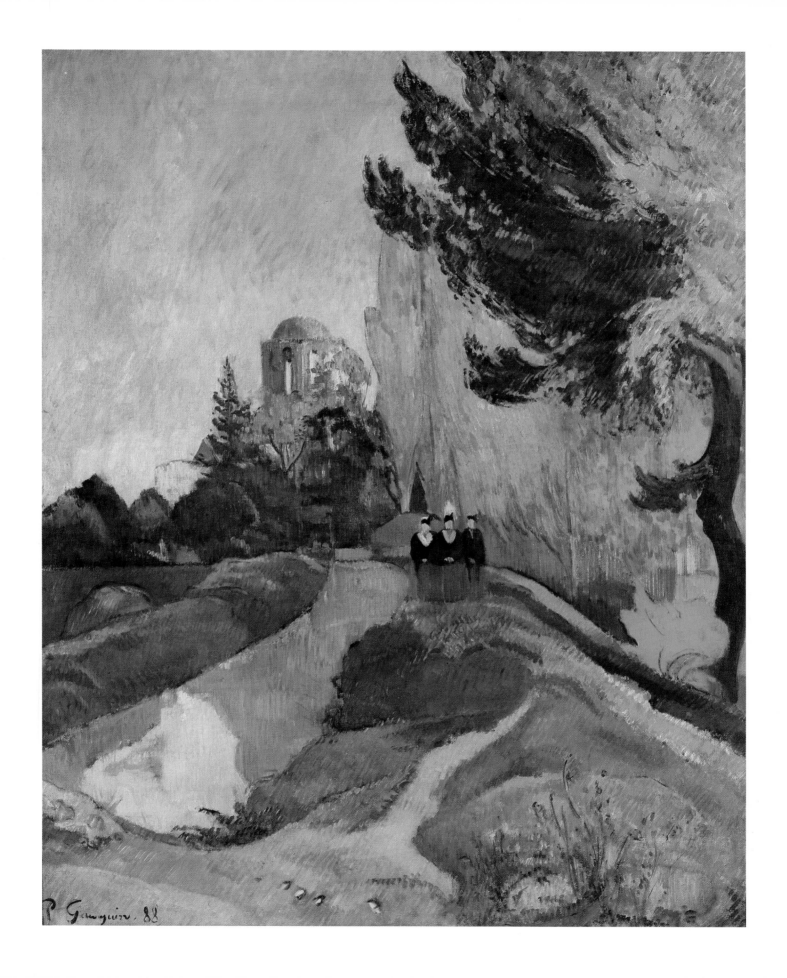

Paul GAUGUIN (1848–1903)

Les meules jaunes, or La moisson blonde

(*Yellow Haystacks* or *The Golden Harvest*), 1889

Oil on canvas, $28\frac{3}{4} \times 36\frac{1}{4}$ (73 × 92)

Gift of Mme Huc de Monfreid, 1951 (R.F. 1951–6)

This canvas was painted after the Arles episode and Gauguin's confrontation with Van Gogh during the painter's third visit to Brittany in the summer of 1889. A brief sojourn in Paris, where the Eiffel Tower was arousing strong feelings and lively debate, in the setting of the International Exhibition, had enabled Gauguin to show the Parisian public a selection from his earlier work. However, the Café Volpini show, where work by Gauguin's friends who were as yet unknown – among them Schuffenecker, Laval, Bernard and Anquetin – hung side by side with his own productions, met almost nothing but incomprehension. He thus returned to Brittany disappointed; and this time chose to settle at the little village of La Pouldu, not far from Pont-Aven. He took up residence at the inn kept by Marie Henry, also known as Marie the Doll, who is immortalized in portraits left to us by Gauguin and his friends.

Breaking finally with the Impressionism with which he had begun his career (*La Seine au pont d'Iéna*, 1875) and which can still be felt in his earlier Breton works (*Les lavandières à Pont-Aven* [*The Washerwomen at Pont-Aven*], 1886), Gauguin now turned firmly towards an idealist – or 'synthetist', as he himself called it – method of painting, freed from the constraints of naturalism which then prevailed in the official Salons. Brittany, far from the hurly-burly of Paris, was a region where it was still possible to live cheaply, and a land whose traditions were still alive, and where an archaic way of life was still a reality. Gauguin often returned to the theme of haystacks – a theme which was particularly popular with the members of the Pont-Aven School. Here the huge mass of the rick invades a strongly constructed picture-space, and seen against it are the silhouettes of two Breton women in traditional costume. The stylistic direction taken here is in complete opposition to that of Impressionism. In order to be convinced of this, one has only to look at the famous paintings of haystacks by Monet, of which the Jeu de Paume has a fine example dating from 1891.   CF-T

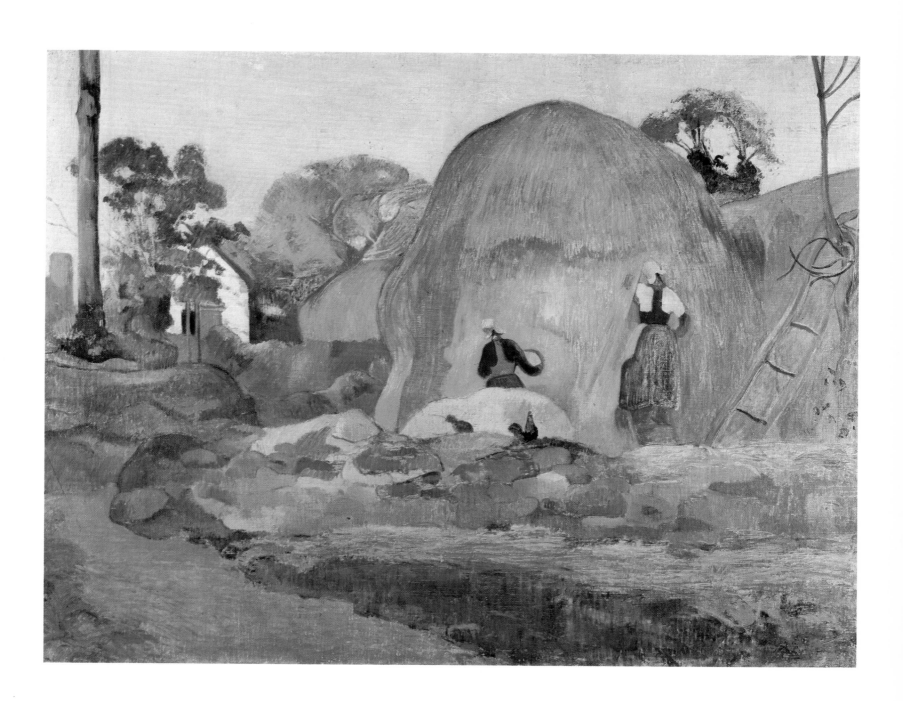

Paul GAUGUIN (1848–1903)

Le repas (*The Meal*), 1891

Oil on canvas-backed paper, $28\frac{3}{8} \times 36\frac{1}{4}$ (72×92)

Gift of M. and Mme André Meyer, but retained by the donors for their lifetimes, 1954; retention abandoned, 1975 (R.F. 1954–27)

Gauguin's period in Brittany was followed in 1891 by escape and voluntary exile in Tahiti. In rebellion against a public which did not understand the first thing about his art, in flight from material and family problems, disgusted with civilization and spurning odious realism in art – everything encouraged him to cast off his moorings. By suggesting he read Pierre Loti, Van Gogh was certainly responsible in great measure for sending Gauguin to this island where he hoped to find the lost Eden of his dreams. *Le repas*, also described in one of the painter's Tahitian notebooks as *Nature morte fei* (*Fei Still-life*, *fei* being Tahitian for 'banana'), is one of the first pictures he produced after his arrival. Its plastic and decorative qualities make it also one of the finest, and show clearly that Gauguin's art had found its true stature in the tropics. In the foreground, occupying two-thirds of the table which is rhythmically divided into horizontal bands, is a splendid still-life full of tropical savour, where blue shadows emphasise the colours. A native drinking-bowl is prominent in the centre. (In a showcase beside the picture there is a similar bowl carved by Gauguin himself, which once belonged to the celebrated dealer Vollard.) Even seen in isolation, this detail shows that Gauguin was Cézanne's equal in defining space and volume by means of colour. The frieze-like composition, and the faces of the three fascinated children, give this work a powerful, enigmatic allure.

CF-T

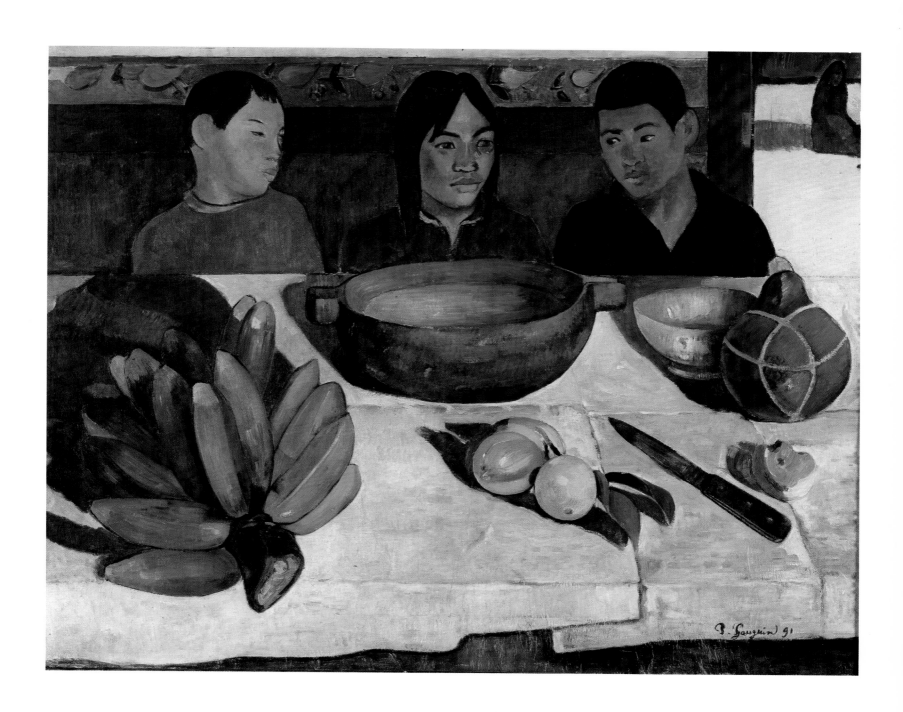

Paul GAUGUIN (1848–1903)

Femmes de Tahiti or *Sur la plage* (*Tahitian Women* or *On the Beach*), 1891

Oil on canvas, 27⅛ × 35⅞ (69 × 91)
Viscount Guy du Cholet bequest, 1923 (R.F. 2765)

'It's always silent. I can understand how these people pass hours and days seated, in melancholy contemplation of the sky. I feel all this beginning to invade me', wrote Gauguin in July 1891 to his wife Mette, who had taken refuge in Denmark with her family. It was through Tahitian women, his successive mistresses, that the artist became increasingly aware of the indolent and melancholy charm of the Polynesian soul. This painting, contemporary with *La repas* (p. 60), and also with his finest Tahitian portraits such as the famous *Vahine no te tiare* (*The Woman with the Flower*) in Copenhagen, offers a splendid image of a way of life which was as vegetative as it was difficult to break free of. The picture obeys the same compositional rules as *Le repas*, in the way that it links broad, space-denying horizontal bands with the two large figures in the foreground – a scheme already fully worked out by the artist during his years in Brittany. The Tahitian motif of the flowered *pareo* reinforces the decorative effect made by this canvas, which the artist enlivens with bold colour harmonies. The chaste attitudes of his Tahitian women here contrast with the tempting sensuality of those in a picture hanging near it, aptly entitled *Et l'or de leur corps* (*And the Gold of Their Bodies*). CF-T

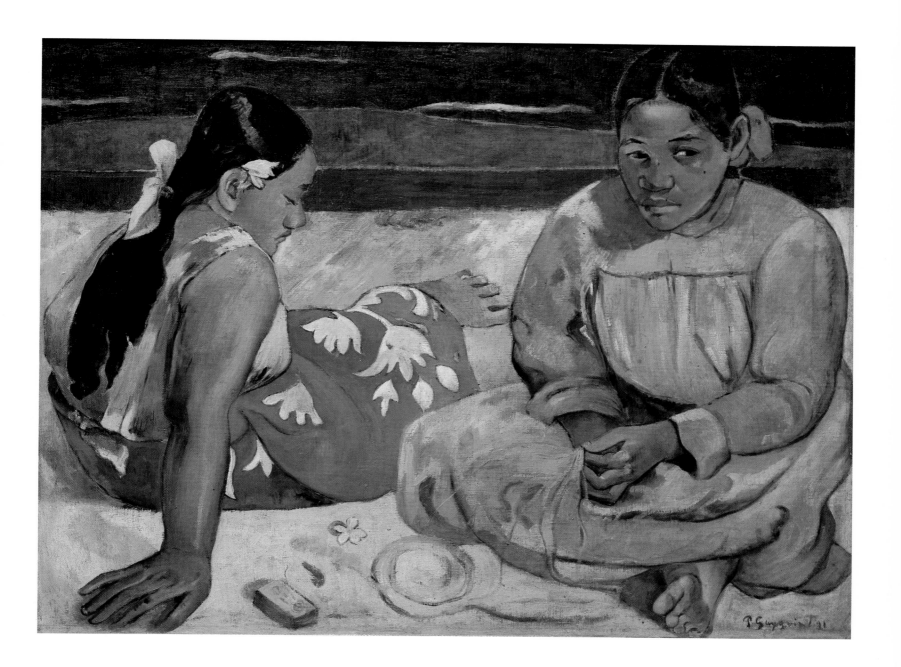

Paul GAUGUIN (1848–1903)

Portrait de l'artiste (*Self-portrait*), c. 1893–94

Oil on canvas, $18\frac{1}{8} \times 15$ (46×38)

Purchased in 1966 (R.F. 1966–7)

Gauguin, Van Gogh and Cézanne, in contrast to Impressionist painters such as Monet, Renoir and Sisley, are among the artists most pre-occupied with their own image, which they treat in their own different ways. The Jeu de Paume has important self-portraits by each of them, revealing as much about their attitudes towards themselves as about their pictorial experimentation. On the one hand there is the anguished introspection of Van Gogh – of which his *Self-portrait* of 1889 (see p. 150) is a moving example – and on the other, the lofty, refined compositions of Gauguin, always concerned with symbolic allusions, and the solid constructions of Cézanne. In addition to the *Self-portrait* of c. 1893 illustrated here, which was completed after Gauguin's first return to Paris from Tahiti, the Jeu de Paume has another, painted earlier and dedicated to his friend Daniel de Monfreid, in which the painter shows himself in profile.

Following the classic tradition, Gauguin liked to show himself against a background containing paintings of his own for which he felt a particular affection. Recognizable in the background here is *Manau Tupapu* (*The Spirits of the Dead Keep Watch*), painted in Tahiti in 1892. Gauguin had previously painted himself in 1889 in front of his famous *Christ jaune* (*Yellow Christ*). There were two good reasons for doing so: in all modesty he thought of himself as the new Christ of painting, and considered this work to be in the front rank of his Breton experiments. Van Gogh, Carrière and Charles Morice were all of them the dedicatees of self-portraits with symbolic messages. In this one, on the back of which is a portrait of his Parisian neighbour the composer William Molard, Gauguin postures arrogantly in an extravagant costume which tells one a great deal about his theatrical temperament. The almost sculptural force of the painting makes it one of the most important images of the artist. CF-T

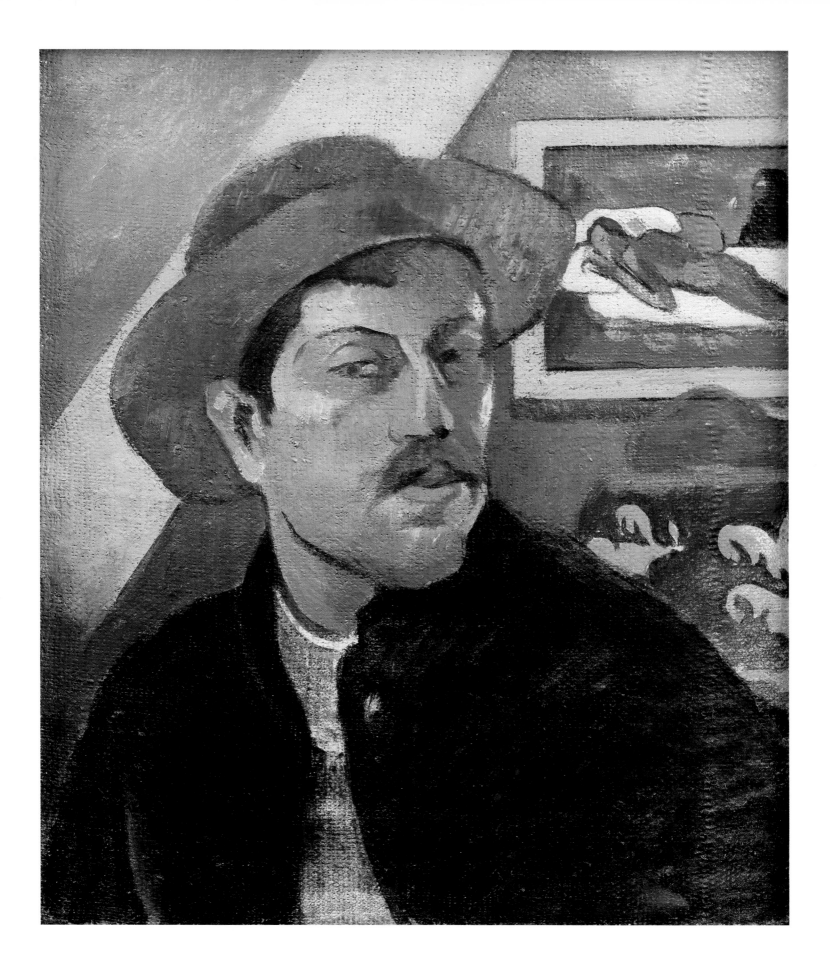

Paul GAUGUIN (1848–1903)

Paysannes bretonnes (*Breton Peasant Women*), 1894

Oil on canvas, 26 × 36¼ (66 × 92)

Gift of Max and Rosy Kaganovitch, 1973 (R.F. 1973–17)

This canvas dates from 1894, that is from after Gauguin's first period in Tahiti, and thus may represent a return to the past, a new pilgrimage to his Breton roots. This seems likely from the fact that Gauguin has returned to one of his favourite subjects at the time of his visits to Le Pouldu and Pont-Aven in earlier years. The left-hand side of the picture, with a man bending towards the ground and two immobile silhouettes in traditional costume, recalls Gauguin's earliest Breton landscapes, and what was borrowed from him by his colleagues Emile Bernard, Paul Sérusier and Jacob Meyer de Haan. There is the same strictly constructed landscape, and a similar opposition of flat zones of colour. But if the two women – who are presumably Breton – are wearing local headdress, their features and postures are nevertheless far more evocative of the Tahitians Gauguin had already immortalized than they are of the rustic inhabitants of the Breton countryside, as depicted for instance in his zinc etchings of the Le Pouldu period. Even the landscape to the right has exotic resonances and mingles Tahitian touches with memories of Gauguin's first voyage to Martinique in 1887.

It must be said that Gauguin hardly found this last visit to Brittany inspiring. He dreamed only of one thing: 'In December', he wrote, 'I am going back [to Paris], and I shall spend every day trying to sell all I possess . . . Once I've got the money in my pocket I'm leaving for Oceania. Nothing will stop me going, and I'm leaving forever.'

This picture, like Monet's *L'église de Vétheuil* (see p. 100), formed part of the important Kaganovitch gift which enriched the Jeu de Paume with numerous Impressionist and Post-Impressionist works. (Paintings by Cézanne and Pissarro among the former, and by Bonnard, Derain and Vlaminck among the latter.) CF-T

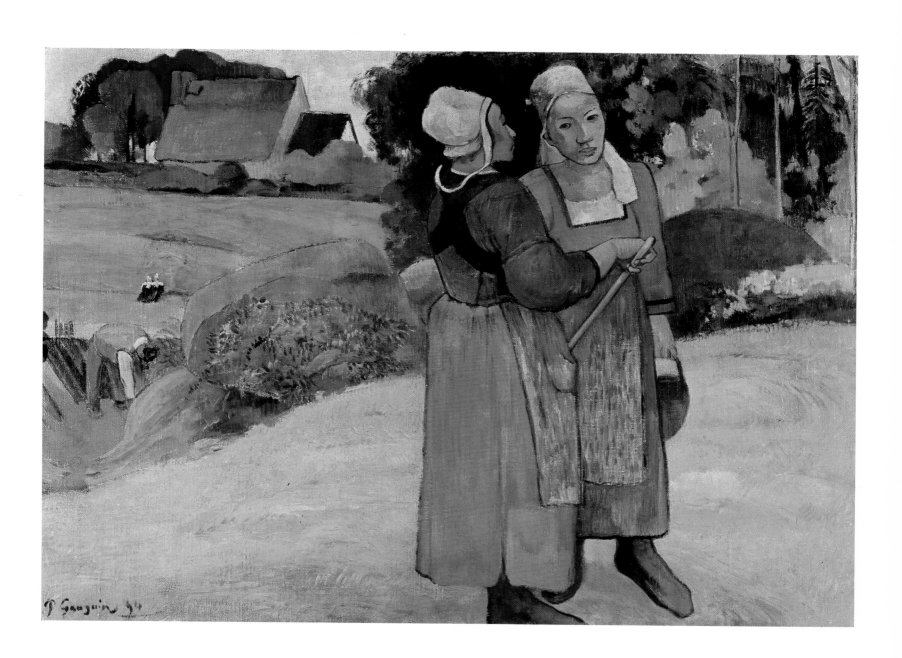

Paul GAUGUIN (1848–1903)

Vairumati, 1897

Oil on canvas, $28\frac{3}{4} \times 37$ (73 × 94)

Formerly Matsukata Collection. Ceded to the Louvre under the terms of the peace treaty with Japan, 1959 (R.F. 1959–5)

At the end of 1898, Gauguin sent this picture from Tahiti, where he had settled once again in 1895, to the Parisian dealer Ambroise Vollard. 'The dream which brought me to Tahiti has been cruelly shattered by present circumstances; it was the Tahiti of former times which I loved, and I couldn't resign myself to the idea that it was entirely extinguished, that this beautiful race had preserved none of its splendour', wrote Gauguin in *Noa-Noa*. If we are to judge by this work, it would seem that he sublimated his disappointment in painting, as the Tahitian dream here becomes flesh in a warm harmony of red and ochre. The heroine of the canvas is the beautiful Vairumati (Gauguin's misspelling of the Tahitian name Vairaumati) who was a legendary being among the Tahitians of Ariois. She was said to have attracted the great Oro to earth and thus to have become the mother of the Ariois race, masters of the island in prehistoric times. Gauguin thus describes her in *Noa-Noa*: 'She was tall, and the fires of the sun shone in the gold of her flesh, while all the mysteries of love slept in the night of her hair.' Her image re-appears, with the symbolic bird, in the large triptych in the Boston Museum of Fine Arts, *D'où venons-nous? Que sommes-nous? Où allons-nous? (Where have we come from? What are we? Where are we going?)*. The sculptures of the Javanese temple of Borobudur probably supplied Gauguin with the inspiration for the two female figures in the background. CF-T

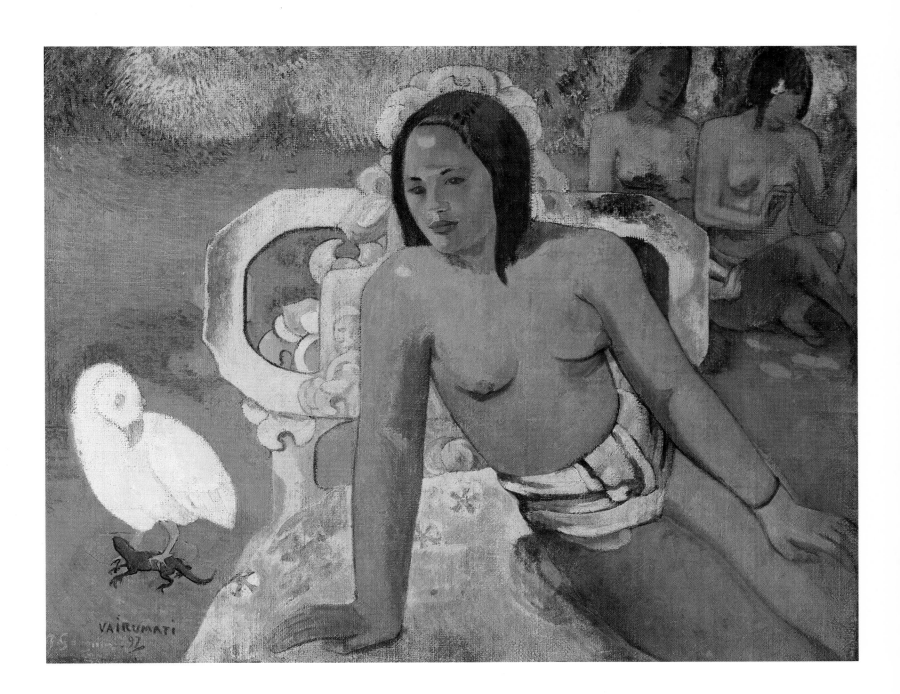

Paul GAUGUIN (1848–1903)

Le cheval blanc (*The White Horse*), 1898

Oil on canvas, $55\frac{1}{8} \times 35\frac{7}{8}$ (140×91)
Purchased 1927 (R.F. 2616)

'But the horse is green! Horses like that don't exist!' exclaimed the man for whom this picture was intended, a pharmacist insensitive to its strange poetry, and who therefore refused to accept it. *Le cheval blanc* thus went to join other Tahitian paintings which Gauguin had already sent to his faithful friend Daniel de Monfreid. The latter spared no effort to sell Gauguin's work in Paris, so as to send financial help to the artist, who was always in desperate need of money. Finally Monfreid offered the painting to the French national collections, and thus it became part of the museum of modern art of that epoch – the Musée du Luxembourg.

Long misunderstood, this painting is nevertheless one of the artist's finest Tahitian works, the decorative effect and the strangeness of the content being wonderfully combined in a richly coloured symphony. Original though it is, the painting has its roots in the purest antique tradition. Gauguin took the stance of the horse from the west frieze of the Parthenon, of which he possessed old collotype photographs, while the tree betrays the Japanese influence which is already to be felt in paintings of the Breton period. There are also affinities with several paintings of horses by Degas, which Gauguin much admired. These different iconographic sources are inextricably intermingled with local Polynesian mythology, where the white horse was a symbol of the sacred.   CF-T

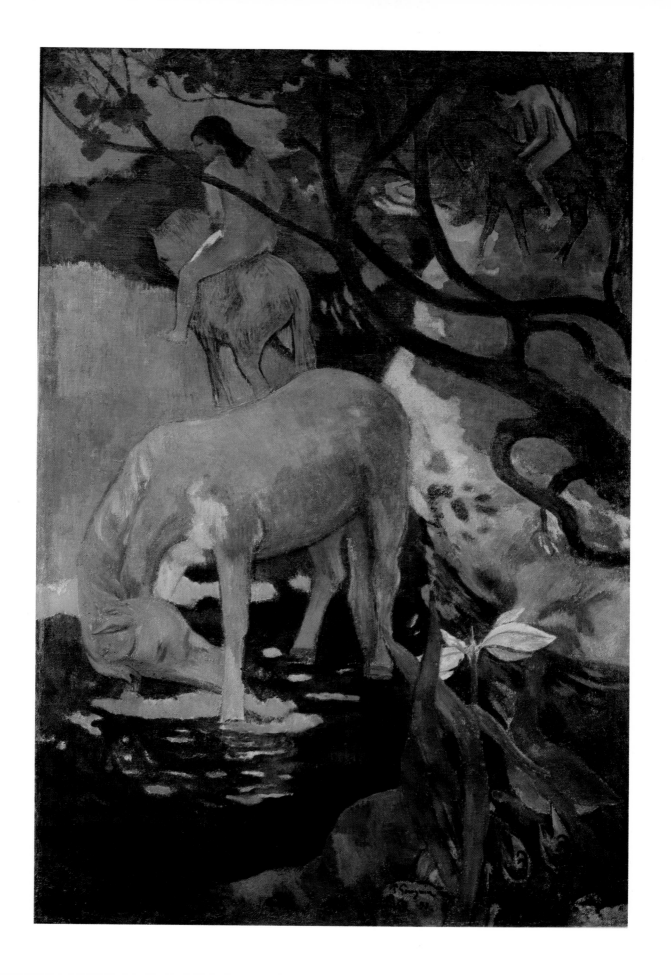

Edouard MANET (1832–1883)

Portrait de M. et Mme Auguste Manet, 1860

Oil on canvas, $45\frac{1}{2} \times 35\frac{7}{8}$ (115.5 × 91)

Purchased with the help of the Rouart family, of Mme J. Weil Picard and of an anonymous foreign donor, 1977 (R.F. 1977–12)

After six years study in the studio of Thomas Couture – which included several clashes with the master – and after having visited numerous European museums, Manet submitted his first painting, *Buveur d'absinthe* (*Absinthe-drinker*), to the Salon of 1859. It was rejected. In 1861, at the next Salon, he had two works accepted and was given an honourable mention. The *Chanteur espagnol* (*Spanish Singer*) aroused the admiration of a group of realist painters, among them Fantin-Latour, Legros and Carolus-Duran, but this portrait of his parents was found disconcerting and was badly received by many people. It was considered vulgar and over-realistic. Jacques-Emile Blanche reports that a friend of Mme Manet's said that 'they look like two concierges'.

Manet portrays his parents in their dining-room, in the clothes they would normally wear at home. Depicted two years before his death, his father, who was an important magistrate and a judge at the court of appeal, looks strained and ageing. His wife was only fifty at the time of the portrait, and was to survive both her husband and her son. She seems uneasy, and is busy with her embroidery wools – they add a rare touch of colour in this dark, austere picture – choosing threads with which to continue her work which lies to the right on the table. The painting evokes the severe and strict way of life of an upper-middle-class couple at the time of the Second Empire, and makes this as striking a reflection of the society of that period as Ingres' *Portrait of M. Bertin* is of the July Monarchy of Louis-Philippe.

As so often, Manet worked on this painting for a long time. Treatment with X-rays has shown that his father was originally shown looking younger, without a moustache and with a less bushy beard.

GL

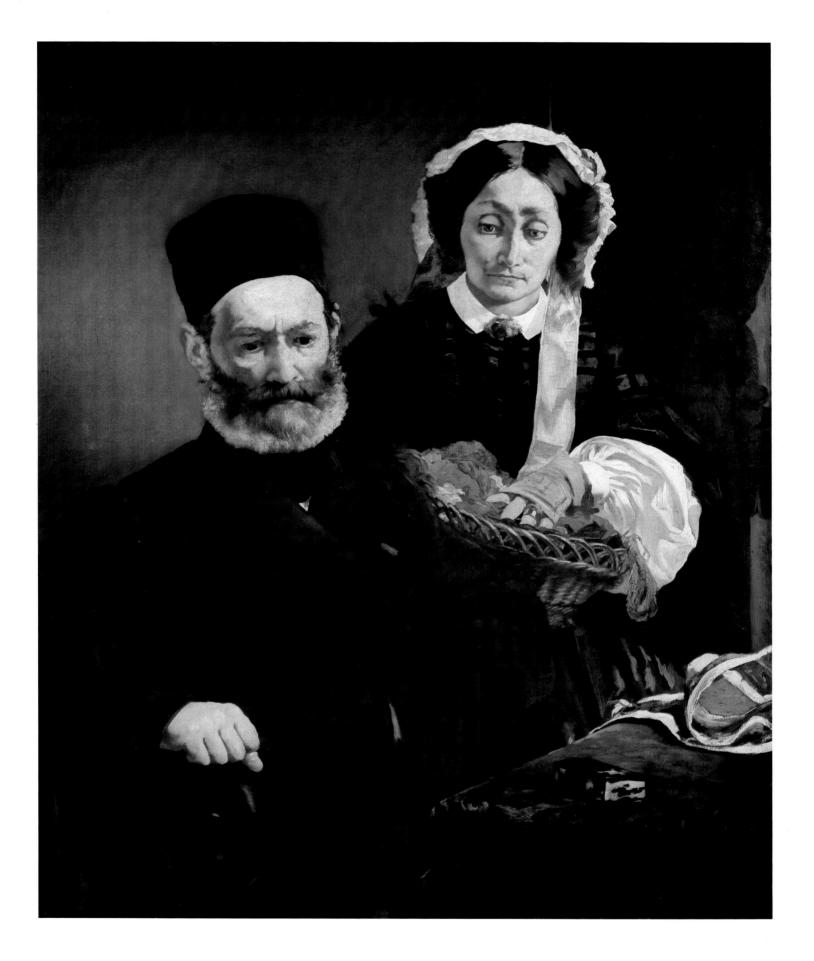

Edouard MANET (1832–1883)

Le déjeuner sur l'herbe (Luncheon on the Grass), 1863

Oil on canvas, $81\frac{7}{8} \times 104$ (208 × 264)

Gift of Etienne Moreau-Nélaton, 1906 (R.F. 1668)

On 1 January 1867 Emile Zola wrote: '*Le déjeuner sur l'herbe* is Manet's greatest picture, the one in which he has realized a dream common to all painters, that of putting life-size figures into a landscape setting.' The landscape itself – a light-filled forest interior with a river – was something Manet had already attempted a little earlier, in *La pêche* (*Fishing*, New York, Metropolitan Museum). The boat in that picture reappears in this composition, which is made up of studies done at Saint-Ouen on the Seine near Manet's country house at Gennevilliers, together with memories of landscapes by Carracci and Rubens.

The Old Master sources for *Le déjeuner sur l'herbe* are well known, notably the *Concert champêtre* by Titian in the Louvre (at that time being attributed to Giorgione) and Marcantonio Raimondi's engraving (then well known in artists' studios) after Raphael's *Judgment of Paris*. But it looks as if Manet also wanted to set himself up as the rival of Courbet, to surpass him in the presentation of subjects drawn from everyday life by producing works even more daring than Courbet's *Baigneuses* (*Women Bathing*, Musée de Montpellier) which was shown at the Salon of 1853, or his *Demoiselles des bords de la Seine* (*Young Ladies on the Banks of the Seine*, Petit Palais, Paris), with their suggestive déshabille, which was shown at the Salon of 1857.

For *Le déjeuner sur l'herbe*, Manet had young people of his own day adopt exactly the same poses as the figures in Raimondi's engraving. And just as Titian's figures wear contemporary sixteenth-century costume, so too these wear the fashions of their time. In the centre is the Dutch sculptor Ferdinand Leenhoff, brother of Manet's mistress Suzanne; seen in profile is one of his brothers. The seated nude is Victorine Meurent, who had been Manet's favourite model for the past year. She is obviously a model resting, just about to put her clothes on again, and not the ideal figure that Cabanel, Baudry or Amaury-Duval would have been painting at that period.

A fortnight later, in the neighbouring galleries of the Palais de l'Industrie, the opening of the Salon des Refusés took place, having been set up at Napoleon III's behest to compensate for the severity of that year's jury of academicians. Here Manet enjoyed a *succès de scandale* with his picture, then entitled *Le bain* (*The Bath*). It was shocking because of its subject – Manet himself simply described it as a 'foursome' – and equally so for its breadth of handling. This made it seem like a sketch, except for the lower left-hand corner, which is treated as a virtuoso still-life. GL

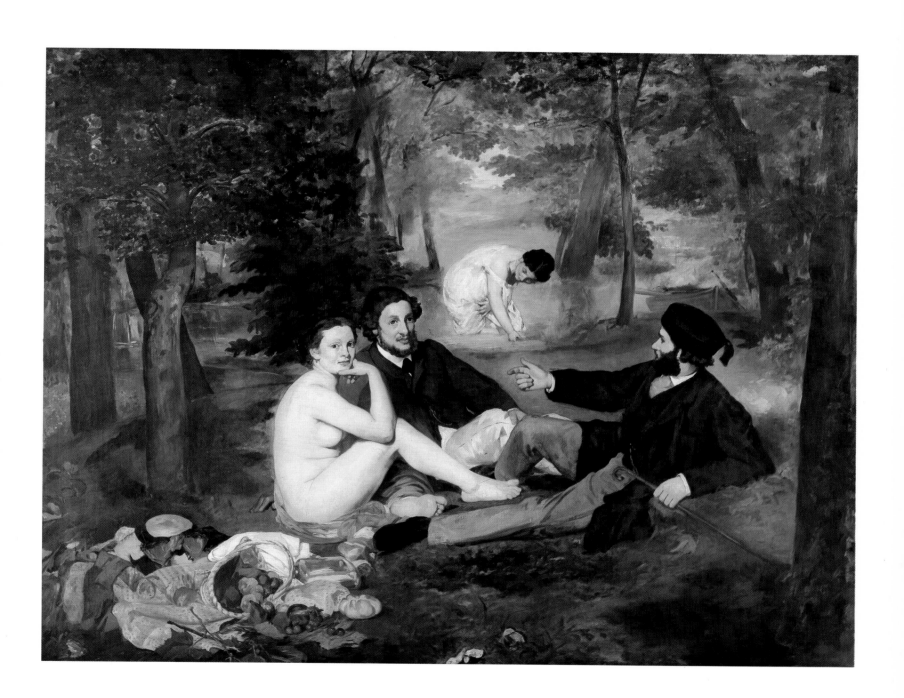

Edouard MANET (1832–1883)

Olympia, 1863

Oil on canvas, $51\frac{3}{8} \times 74\frac{3}{4}$ (130.5 × 190)

Donated to the national collections through public subscription initiated by Claude Monet, 1890 (R.F. 644)

Like *Le déjeuner sur l'herbe*, Manet's *Olympia* is now recognized worldwide as one of the classic masterpieces of art, and has been the inspiration of modern artists, ranging from Cézanne (see p. 24) to Picasso and Larry Rivers. It is on a par with Ingres' *Grande odalisque*, and was hung side by side with it at the Louvre in 1907. In the Salon of 1865, however, when it was first shown, it aroused an unprecedented scandal and more or less general hilarity. The drawing was criticized, the shadows were 'like streaks of shoe-blacking' according to Théophile Gautier, and the painter's claim that he wished to represent 'an aristocratic young woman' (the phrase comes from the poem by Zacharie Astruc which accompanied the enigmatic title in the Salon catalogue) was flatly disbelieved. People saw the woman as a contemporary model taking a pose, a realistically depicted nude, a prostitute staring at the spectator while her black servant brings her a bouquet sent by one of her clients.

Manet wanted to confront the masters of the past once again with this picture, while at the same time parodying a theme which occurred frequently in the Salons of the nineteenth century. The obvious historical source is Titian's *Venus of Urbino*, which Manet copied in Florence, here using the general scheme of the composition as well as the pose; the arrogance and insolence he borrows from Goya's *Maja desnuda* (*Naked Maja*). But he has transposed his models into a naturalistic key, painting – as his friend Antonin Proust reports – what he actually saw. Contemporaries were shocked by the striking contrasts, the flat colour, and were not attuned to the classic harmony of the composition, nor to the refinement of the whites, ivories and rosy hues, nor to the richness of the background, which has now been revealed once again by recent restoration. They were blind to the virtuosity of the bouquet composed of just a few splashes of colour, its reds echoing Olympia's ribbon and the flowers on the shawl – in fact to everything which now appears to us as a demonstration of the pleasure Manet took in painting with such skill. GL

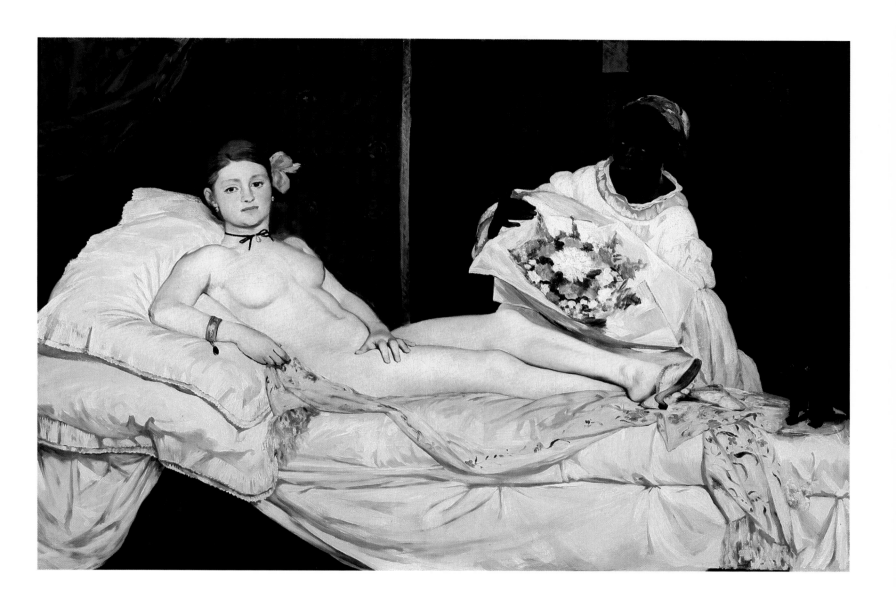

Edouard MANET (1832–1883)

Le fifre (*The Fifer*), 1866

Oil on canvas, 63 × 38⅝ (160 × 98)

Count Isaac de Camondo bequest, 1911 (R.F. 1992)

The young model is a 'fifer of the light infantrymen of the Guard' – a boy-soldier who was a member of the troop of the Imperial Guard quartered at the La Pepinière barracks. He was brought to Manet by his friend Commandant Lejosne, Bazille's uncle. Like Manet's *L'acteur tragique* (*Tragic Actor* – a portrait of Rouvière in the role of Hamlet, rejected as was the present picture at the Salon of 1866, and now in the National Gallery of Art, Washington DC), *Le fifre* was done in homage to the art of Velásquez, which had so impressed and delighted him when he saw it at the Prado, during his trip to Spain in August 1865. He seems to be defining his own approach when he writes to Fantin-Latour, describing a work by the man he called the 'quintessential painter': 'The most outstanding painting in his marvellous œuvre, and perhaps the most astonishing ever painted, is the one the catalogue calls *Portrait of a Famous Actor of the Time of Philip IV*. The background disappears. It's pure atmosphere which surrounds the figure, which is dressed from head to foot in black and totally alive.'

Zola, who was brought to Manet's studio by the painter Guillemet, soon afterwards had an enthusiastic article published in *L'Evénement* on 7 May 1866, which led to his own dismissal from the paper. Writing about *Le fifre*, he said: 'I don't believe it is possible to get a more powerful effect by simpler means. M. Manet is brusque – he tackles things directly. He is not put off by the brusqueness of nature; he passes from black to white without hesitation. He renders with vigour the contrast between different objects, one separated from the other.'

Manet was accused of having painted a crude popular print, a playing-card picture, because of the sharp contrast of red and black on a grey ground, with a few touches of acid yellow so typical of him. In fact he was paying tribute, not only to Spain, but to the unmodulated blacks in the Japanese prints he then admired.   GL

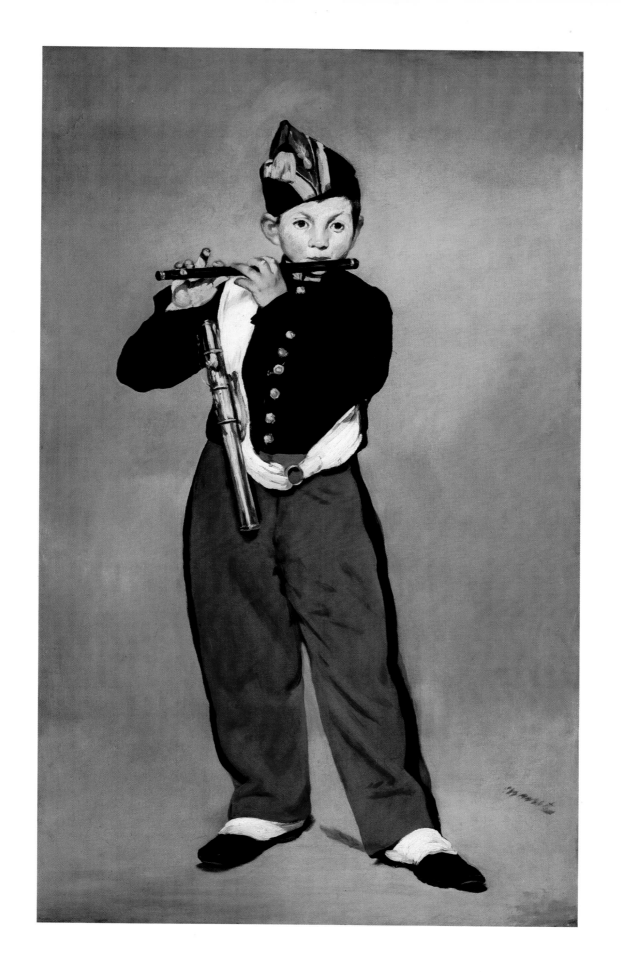

Edouard MANET (1832–1883)

Portrait d'Emile Zola, 1868

Oil on canvas, $57\frac{1}{2} \times 44\frac{7}{8}$ (146×114)

Gift of Mme Emile Zola but retained by her for her lifetime, 1918; entered the Louvre in 1925 (R.F. 2205)

The naturalistic novelist Emile Zola, who was a childhood friend of Cézanne, took an interest in painting from very early on, and defended Manet stoutly when he was rejected by the Salon of 1866. Soon afterwards, Zola further developed his ideas in an article which attracted much attention when it was published in the *Revue du XIXème siècle* on 1 January 1867. It was entitled 'A New Method of Painting. Edouard Manet', and was reprinted as a pamphlet for Manet's one-man show in the Place de l'Alma, which was timed to coincide with the International Exhibition of 1867. As a gesture of thanks – and to set the seal on a relationship which had developed from admiration to loyal friendship – Manet offered to paint Zola's portrait. He signed it with the title of Zola's celebrated pamphlet, which is placed behind the writer's pen, on the table on the right.

The picture was probably begun in November 1867, and did not exactly go unnoticed at the Salon of 1868; in fact it was the centre of lively controversy. Many criticized the sitter's distant, indifferent expression, and the young Odilon Redon saw in it 'something more like a still-life than the expression of a man's character'.

It is clear that Manet scrupulously worked out, within a framework of horizontals and verticals, a setting which would illustrate the interests of both the painter and his critic. Thus the frame high up to the right contains several emblematic images. There is a reproduction – could it be a photograph of an engraving? – of *Olympia* (see p. 76). She gives Zola a look of thanks – he thought the picture Manet's finest masterpiece when he saw it at the Salon of 1865, and described it as 'the complete expression of his temperament'. Above this there is an engraving of *Los Borrachos* (*The Drinkers*), no doubt the one by Nanteuil after Velásquez, which indicates both Manet's admiration for the artist and Zola's penchant for a realism that is 'thick, brutal and violent', to quote Charles Blanc, author of *Histoire des peintres de toutes les écoles*. Zola has one of the illustrated volumes of this on his knees. Finally, there is a print by Utagawa Kuniyaki II, *The Wrestler Onaruto Nadaemon from Awa Province* – an example of the brightly coloured late Ukiyo-e prints which encouraged artists to seek for simplicity and modernity. This print echoes the Japanese screen which is partly visible to the left – a prop often used at this period by other artists who belonged to the same group, such as Whistler, Tissot and Alfred Stevens.   GL

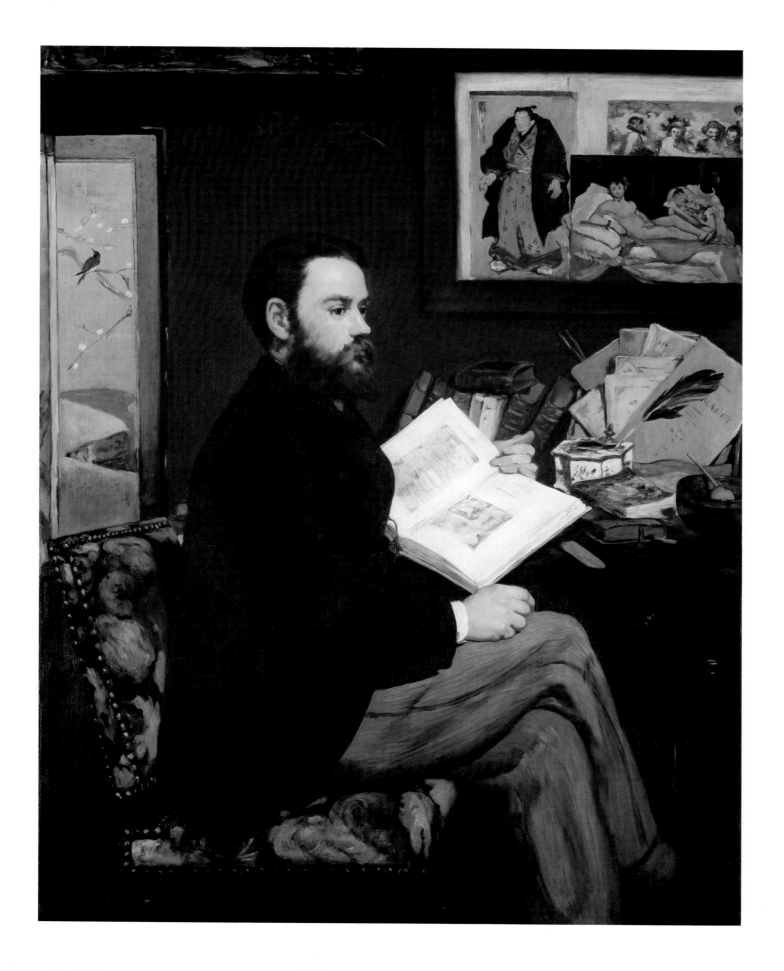

Edouard MANET (1832–1883)

Le balcon (*The Balcony*), 1868–69

Oil on canvas, $66\frac{1}{2} \times 49\frac{1}{4}$ (169×125)
Gustave Caillebotte bequest, 1894 (R.F. 2772)

Manet got the first idea for this painting from a scene he caught sight of during the summer of 1868 at Boulogne-sur-Mer, but the composition itself is one of the final examples of Spanish influence on his art. It was inspired by one of Goya's pictures – the *Majas on a Balcony*, which he may have seen, when he was still an adolescent, in the Spanish collection which belonged to Louis-Philippe, and which had, in any case, just been reproduced (in 1867) in Yriarte's book on Goya. True to his established method, Manet painted the scene from life, during long sessions with the models in his studio in the Rue Guyot in the Batignolles quarter of Paris, during the autumn and winter of 1868–69. The sitters are Berthe Morisot, seated (this being her first appearance in Manet's work); Fanny Claus, a young concert violinist, a friend of the Manet household, and Antoine Guillemet, a landscape painter who was to make an honourable career for himself at the Salon, and who was, on a number of occasions, to come to the help of his Impressionist friends. In the background, the child carrying a jug must be Léon Leenhoff, the boy Manet brought up.

There is nothing left here of Goya's genre scene, with its whispered conversations. It is the image of one particular moment, a sort of snapshot of a scene from contemporary life, where each of the characters is, so to speak, frozen in his or her individual psychology, and does not communicate with the others. The painting disturbed even the theoreticians of naturalism, and aroused a multitude of hostile reactions at the Salon of 1869. The green of the louvred shutters and of the balcony, the brilliant blue of Guillemet's cravat, echoed by the subtler blue of the hydrangea – a kind of emblematic evocation of the open air – the violent contrasts between lights and darks: all these acted as provocation. The painting has not lost its enigmatic power, as Magritte's composition with the same title, done in 1950, confirms. In this work (now in the museum at Ghent) Magritte replaces the three figures with three coffins, one in a seated position.   GL

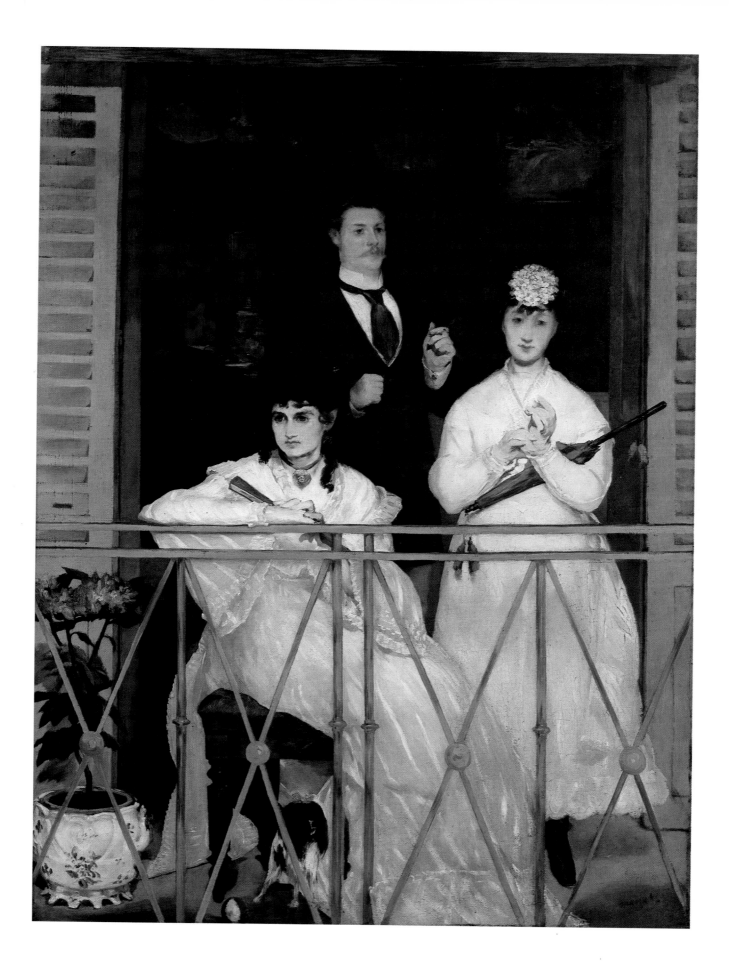

Edouard MANET (1832–1883)

Sur la plage (*On the Beach*), 1873

Oil on canvas, $23\frac{1}{2} \times 28\frac{3}{4}$ (59.6 × 73.2)

Gift of Jean-Edouard Dubrujeaud but retained by him for his lifetime, 1953; entered the Jeu de Paume in 1970 (R.F. 1953–24)

At the time when this was painted, Manet was not only venerated by a small group of artists and writers, but had also started to know better times financially. In 1872 he sold a large number of paintings to the dealer Durand-Ruel, whose meeting with Monet in London in 1871 had led to his interest in the Batignolles group. At the Salon of 1873, Manet had his first major success since 1861, with *Le bon bock* (*The Good Glass of Beer*), a portrait of the print-maker Belot which demonstrates the artist's admiration for Frans Hals, whose work he had seen at Haarlem in 1872. One can detect further reminiscences of Hals in these figures painted from life – as proved by some grains of sand still in the paint – at Berck-sur-Mer. Manet spent a three-week family holiday there in July 1873. His wife Suzanne is recognizable, reading, and also his brother Eugène, lost in thought.

In comparison with Boudin's beach-scenes, or those which Monet did during the same period, Manet endows his figures with exceptional monumentality. Here they occupy the larger part of the canvas; the horizon line is placed very high, and a thin strip of sky is punctuated by the dark sails of some boats. Into this universe of sand and sea, all grey, ochre and blue, Manet introduces as a counterpoint a little touch of red on Madame Manet's shoes in the foreground, which helps to create the brightly lit atmosphere of this northern French beach-scene.   GL

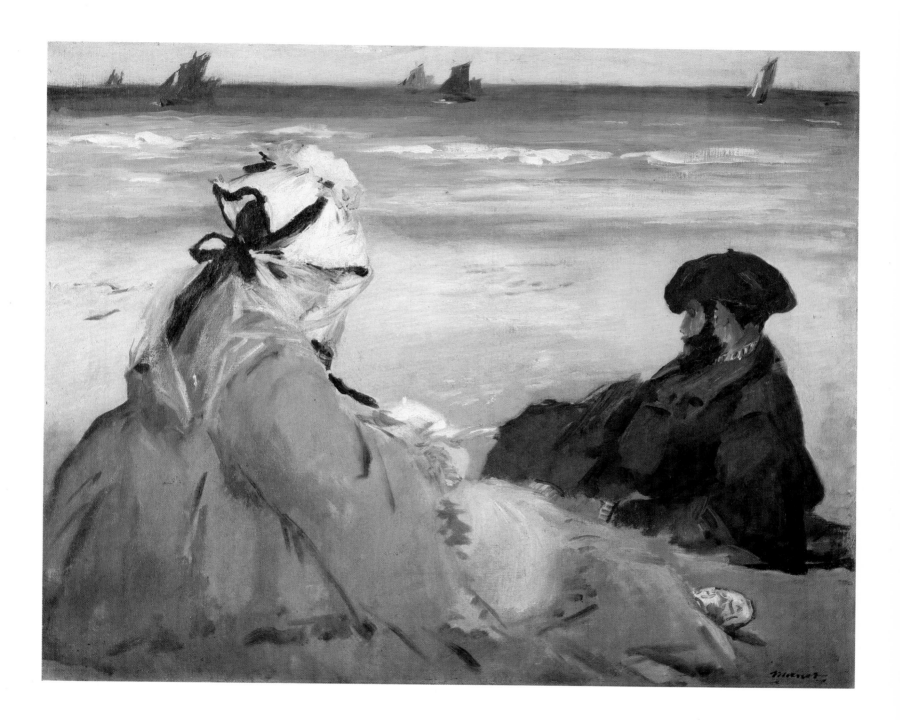

Edouard MANET (1832–1883)

La serveuse de bocks (*The Waitress*), 1879

Oil on canvas, $30\frac{1}{2} \times 25\frac{1}{2}$ (77.5 × 65)

Formerly Matsukata Collection. Ceded to the Louvre under the terms of the peace treaty with Japan, 1959 (R.F. 1959–4)

From 1877–78 onwards Manet, like Degas at this time, was painting numerous café scenes. Drawings made from life were the basis of paintings later constructed in the studio – of which this painting is an important example. It shows the Reichshoffen café-concert, which was probably in the Boulevard Rochechouart in Paris. Manet began work on it in August 1878, but then cut the painting into two parts, which he reworked separately. The right-hand portion, *Coin de café-concert* (*Corner of a Café-concert*, National Gallery, London), corresponds generally to the picture illustrated here. But our painting nevertheless differs in many details, and seems to be a fresh version of the same subject – simplified, better worked out, and arguably later.

Thus the horizontal line of the brightly lit stage is here suppressed to create a tighter composition, punctuated by the verticals of the background which are echoed by those of a top-hat and of the tankards of beer, painted a wonderful orange colour. Many details have disappeared: the musicians in the orchestra and the diagonals made by their instruments, and the table set obliquely and the drinking glasses to the left, have gone – to be replaced by a sort of close-up of characters from many different walks of life, sitting side by side, without knowing each other: a workman in his blue overall, a bourgeois in a top hat, a woman with a high chignon. Above them all rises the waitress. The customers look towards the stage, some more attentively than others, where (on the left of the picture) there appears the long dress and the arm of a singer. But her presence does not concern the waitress going about her work. She deliberately looks towards someone who is invisible – in fact towards the viewer of the painting – thus giving to the painting the reality of life itself.

What one has here is a subtle preparation for the device used in Manet's final masterpiece *Un bar au Folies-Bergère* (*A Bar at the Folies-Bergère*, 1881–82, Courtauld Institute, London). There the man who is speaking to the abstracted and melancholy bar-maid actually appears in the mirror behind her. GL

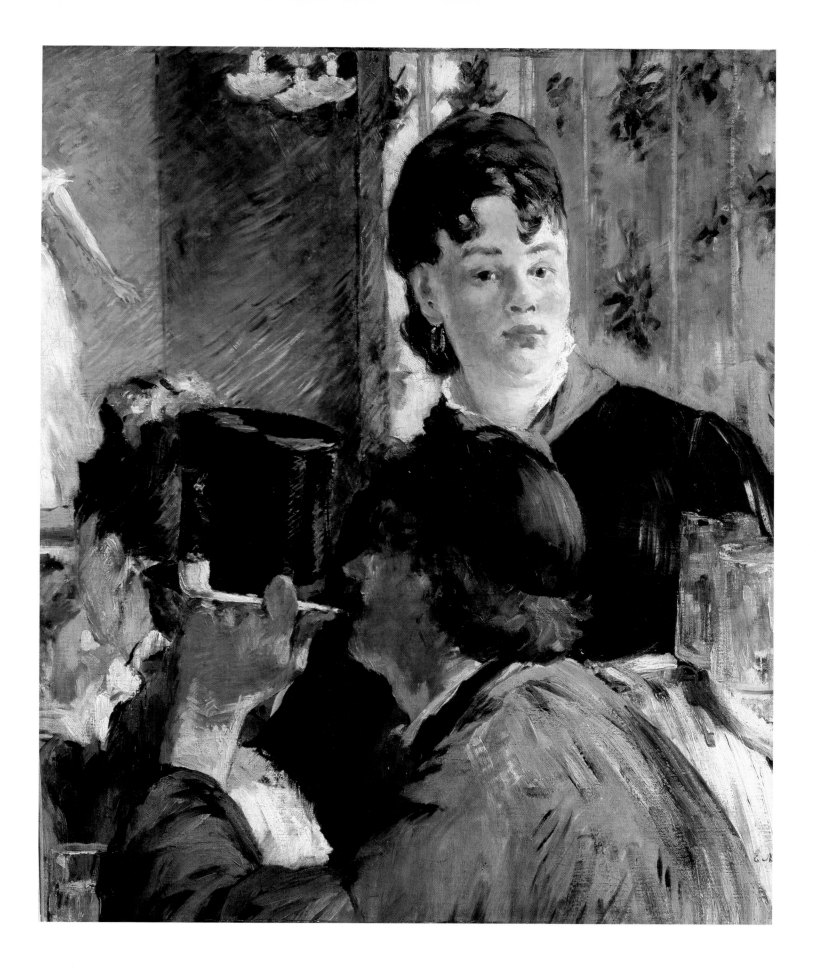

Claude MONET (1840–1926)

Femmes au jardin (*Women in the Garden*), 1866–67

Oil on canvas, $100\frac{3}{8} \times 80\frac{3}{4}$ (255 × 205)
Purchased in 1921 (R.F. 2773)

Claude Monet spent his childhood and youth in Le Havre, where he found his first real teacher, Eugène Boudin, and formed links with the Dutch landscape painter Jongkind. The example set by these two resolutely nonconformist painters decided the direction the young artist was to take. When he arrived in Paris, he joined Gleyre's studio, and there met Bazille, Renoir and probably Sisley. In 1865, he sent two landscapes to the Salon which were favourably received, and had further success the following year with *Camille* (Kunsthalle, Bremen), which was influenced by Courbet and also by Manet. With this to encourage him, Monet started work on a huge composition showing figures in the open air – a second *Déjeuner sur l'herbe*. It was done in homage to Manet, but also perhaps as a challenge to him. He left it unfinished while he turned to painting *Femmes au jardin*. He worked on this at Sèvres, near Paris, and also at Honfleur during the winter of 1866–67.

In order to preserve the freshness of his first sight of the scene in the finished painting, Monet decided to do all the work on it outdoors. This was not an easy matter in view of the huge size of canvas he had chosen. Camille Doncieux, whom he was to marry in 1870, posed for all three figures to the left of the composition, set in a middle-class garden in a Paris suburb. Because of the artist's choice of a 'common' subject (which nevertheless pleased Zola in its modernity), and also because of the technique, which stressed strong contrasts of light and shade and brilliance of colour, the picture was rejected by the jury at the Salon of 1867. This check to his progress aggravated Monet's financial difficulties, and confirmed his position as a dissident. It is worth recalling that the painting belonged first to Bazille, then to Manet, before finding its way back to its author, who, having made his reputation, sold it to the national collections in 1921. AD

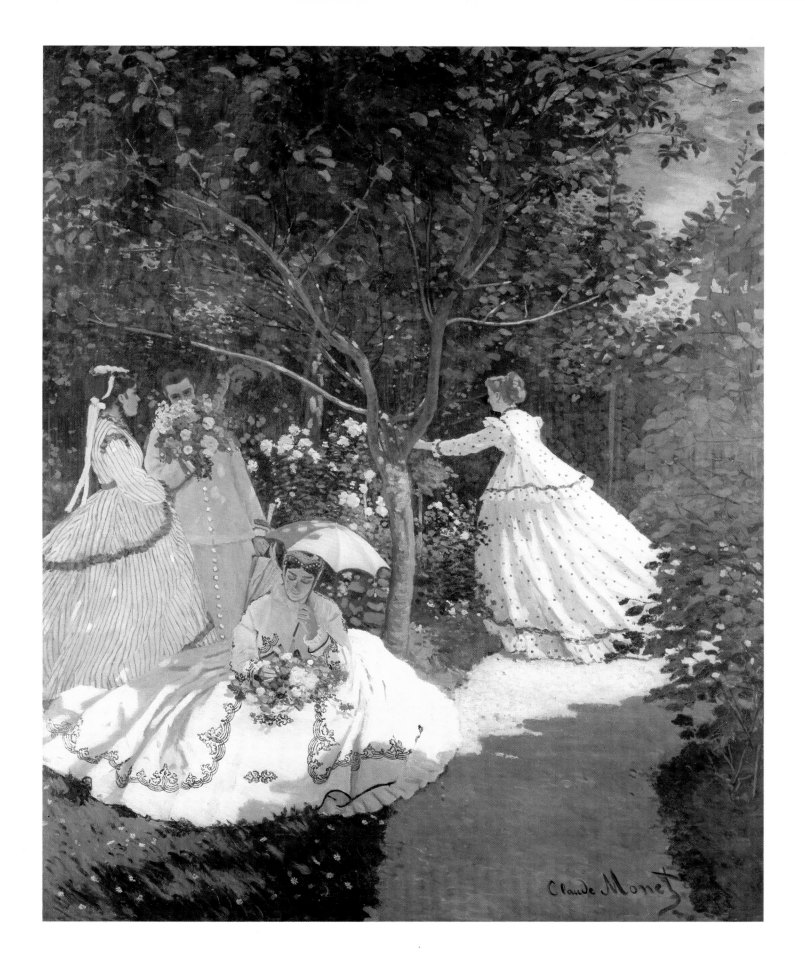

Claude MONET (1840–1926)

L'hôtel des Roches Noires à Trouville

(*The Roches Noires Hotel at Trouville*), 1870

Oil on canvas, $31\frac{1}{2} \times 21\frac{5}{8}$ (80 × 55)

Gift of Jacques Laroche, but retained by him for his lifetime, 1947; entered the Jeu de Paume in 1976

(R.F. 1947–30)

In the 1860s Monet often painted on the Normandy coast in the area around Le Havre, the town where his family lived. When he did this picture at Trouville, he was getting ready to leave France for London after war was declared between France and Prussia. The irony is that the impression of gaiety one immediately gets from the picture is in total contrast with the financial difficulties against which Monet was then struggling, with few collectors interested in his work, which had been officially condemned by repeated rejections at the Paris Salon. In its subject-matter, *L'hôtel des Roches Noires à Trouville* recalls the most seductive works by Boudin, that delightful chronicler of fashionable society at the seaside – Trouville and Deauville being 'launched' under the Second Empire. But in its form it is a wonderful example of Monet's technical virtuosity. With a few vigorous brush-strokes he creates light and shadow, gives life to silhouettes that are just touched in; and with a wide sky in which the wind chases puffs of cloud, he conjures up the seaside freshness of this promenade. The traditional title of the work, *L'hôtel des Roches Noires*, links it to a world evoked considerably later by Proust.   AD

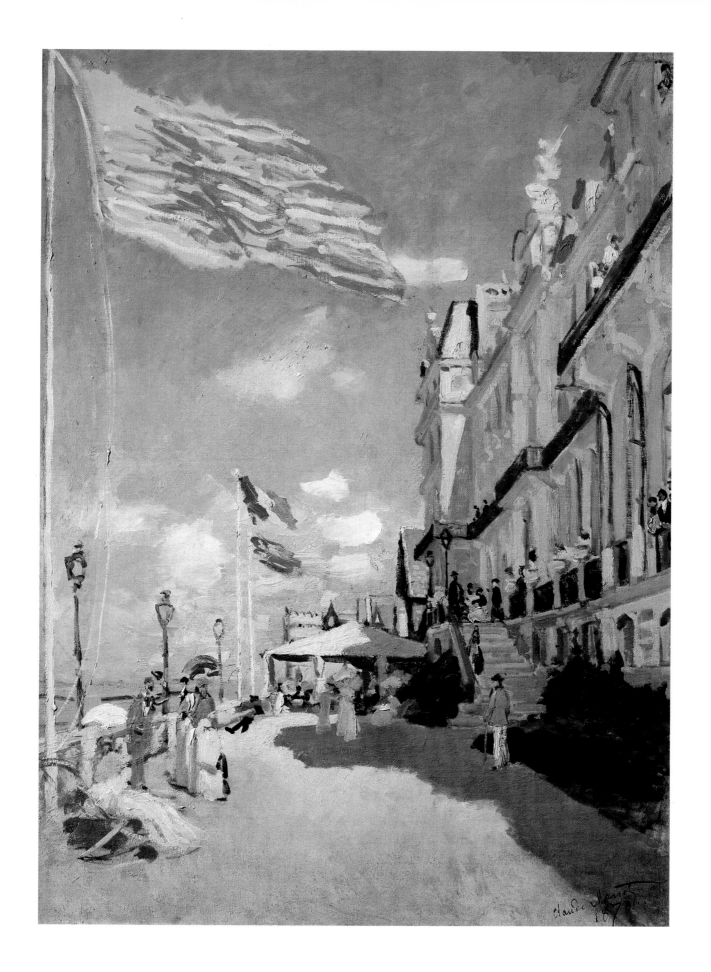

Claude MONET (1840–1926)

Les coquelicots (Wild Poppies), 1873

Oil on canvas, $19\frac{5}{8} \times 25\frac{5}{8}$ (50 × 65)

Gift of Etienne Moreau-Nélaton, 1906 (R.F. 1676)

When he got back from England in the autumn of 1871, Monet lost no time in finding himself somewhere to live at Argenteuil, which was then no more than a largish village on the Seine near Paris. It was frequented chiefly by boating enthusiasts, who sailed their craft on the broad expanse of the river. The name of the village has now become a kind of symbol for the full flowering of Impressionism, not merely because Monet himself found subjects there for numerous brightly lit landscapes – themselves an accomplished statement about things in motion – but also because nearly all the painters linked to the movement came to paint there at his invitation. They included Renoir, Sisley and even Pissarro (who was then living nearby at Pontoise), and above all Manet who, prompted by the example of his young friend, painted some high key works in the open air at Argenteuil on the theme of canoeists.

Les coquelicots was certainly one of the paintings shown at the first Impressionist exhibition of 1874, held in the Boulevard des Capucines in Paris in a building which had been the photographer Nadar's studio. The painting was thus the companion of Monet's famous *Impression, soleil levant* (*Impression: Sunrise*, Musée Marmottan, Paris), whose title, taken up in jest by a hostile critic, was the origin of the term Impressionism. This small picture is a colourist's straightforward reaction to the redness of poppies blooming in a field. Its size contrasts with the large canvases Monet used in the 1860s, and it has preserved all the freshness of a sketch – nevertheless revealing a constant preoccupation with rhythm and balance. The duplication of the group showing a woman with an umbrella and a small child (no doubt they are Monet's wife Camille and his son Jean) suggests movement but also acts as a means of containing the joyous, shimmering colour of the blossoms on the left.

AD

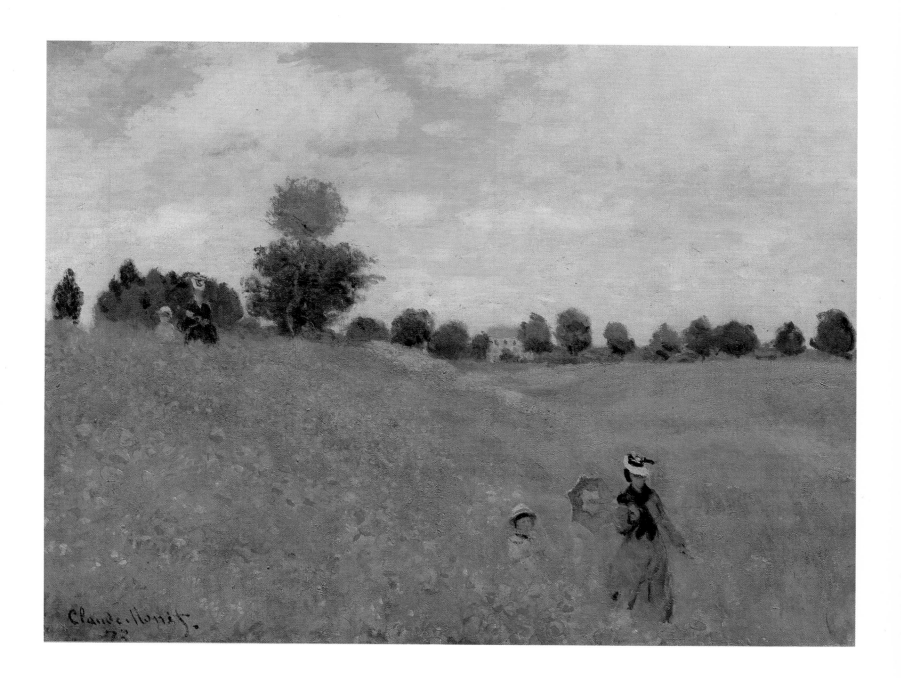

Claude MONET (1840–1926)

Le pont à Argenteuil (*The Bridge at Argenteuil*), 1874

Oil on canvas, $23\frac{5}{8} \times 31\frac{1}{2}$ (60 × 80)

Antonin Personnaz bequest, 1937 (R.F. 1937–41)

One of Monet's favourite themes at Argenteuil was that of sailing-boats on the Seine. Several regatta scenes hang in the Jeu de Paume, but here the boats are moored near the road bridge at Argenteuil, and the artist has concentrated on representing the iridescent surface of the water and the landscape it reflects. The extremely precise technique, despite the apparent freedom of touch, is extremely typical of this period. The years Monet spent at Argenteuil – he lived there until the beginning of 1878 – were a time of stability for him. Contented with his lot, and supported by his dealer Paul Durand-Ruel who was striving tirelessly to widen the still very restricted circle of collectors loyal to the Impressionists, Monet was free to explore the possibilities offered by a kind of high-key painting based on direct observation of a theme in the open air. AD

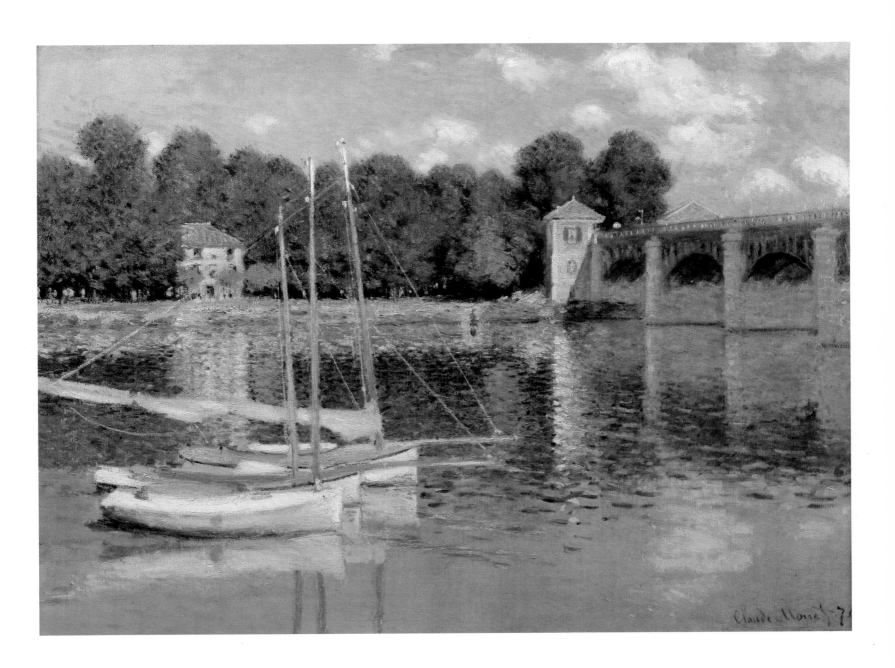

Claude MONET (1840–1926)

La gare Saint-Lazare (*Saint-Lazare Station*), 1877

Oil on canvas, $29\frac{1}{2} \times 41$ (75 × 104)

Gustave Caillebotte bequest, 1894 (R.F. 2775)

In Paris, the terminus for the line from Argenteuil was the Gare Saint-Lazare, and so Monet knew it well. This may in part explain the attraction he felt for this 'contemporary' subject, which had also been attempted by Manet in 1873 in his famous *Le chemin de fer* (*The Railway*, National Gallery of Art, Washington DC). Unlike Manet, and even Gustave Caillebotte who in 1876 painted passers-by on *Le pont de l'Europe* (which was part of the station complex), Monet comes down to the level of the platforms and penetrates the huge canopy of glass and steel which forms the station roof. The human figures are lost amid the coils of white or bluish smoke, which take their colour from the prevailing light conditions. In this respect, the Gare Saint-Lazare series, of which this painting is one, seems to be where the systematic procedure used in his paintings of Rouen cathedral first took shape (pp. 104–07).

Writing about the third Impressionist exhibition of 1877, Zola warmly defended the artist's unorthodox choice of subject: 'This year Monet is showing some wonderful railway station interiors. You can hear the noise of the trains the station swallows up; you see the floods of smoke which unroll under the huge roofs. That's the art of today . . . our painters have been forced to discover the poetry of railway stations, as their fathers discovered that of forests and rivers.' These lines take on their full significance when one recalls that several years later the novelist was to create *La Bête humaine* (published in 1889–90), which was very much a contemporary allegory. AD

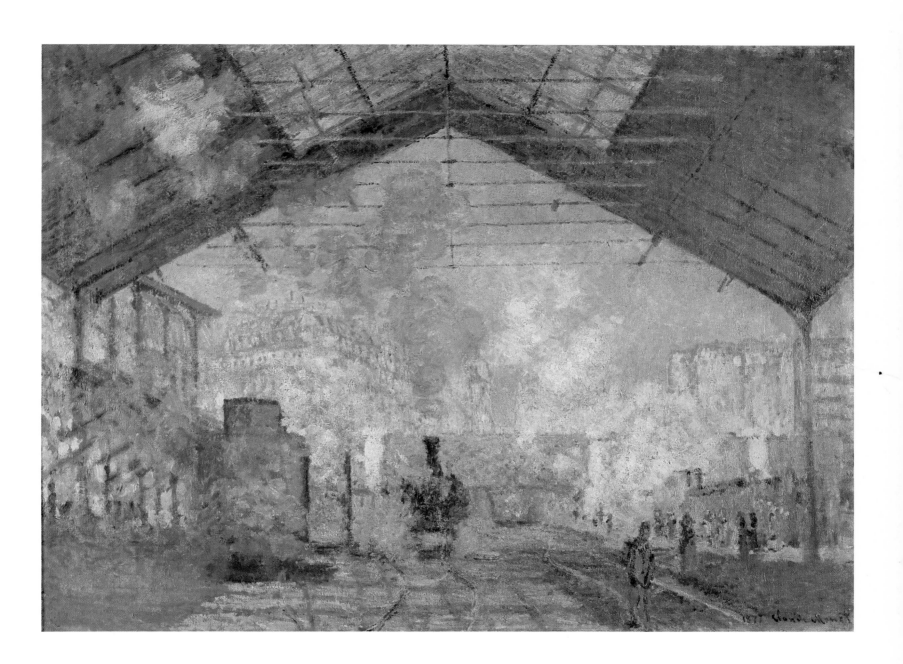

Claude MONET (1840–1926)

La rue Montorgueil : fête du 30 juin 1878
(Rue Montorgueil Decked Out with Flags)

Oil on canvas, $31\frac{1}{2} \times 19\frac{5}{8}$ (80 × 50)

Purchased 1982 (R.F. 1982–71)

Like Manet when he painted his *La rue Mosnier pavoisée* (*Rue Mosnier Decked Out with Flags*, Bührle Collection, Zürich), Monet has here been attracted by the idea of multicoloured flags fluttering in the wind – a theme which later frequently provided inspiration for the Fauves. Most of the Impressionist painters enjoyed painting Paris street-scenes, and here Monet offers one of the earliest examples of a view in perspective taken from a height, of the kind also attempted by Pissarro and Caillebotte. In this painting the dense colours are brought to life by a multitude of closely set brush-strokes. Seen from close to, the picture seems almost entirely abstract; it is only as one steps back that one understands Monet's virtuosity – the composition becomes clear and legible, one becomes aware of the crowd swarming down the street and of the movement of the flags which almost conjures away the presence of the vertical buildings on either side. A very similar picture belongs to the Musée des Beaux-Arts in Rouen, which represents the Rue Saint-Denis on the same day – 30 June 1878 – when the city was hung with flags on the occasion of the International Exhibition. It is thus not in fact a celebration of Bastille Day (14 July), as is sometimes suggested; this did not become a public holiday until later.   AD

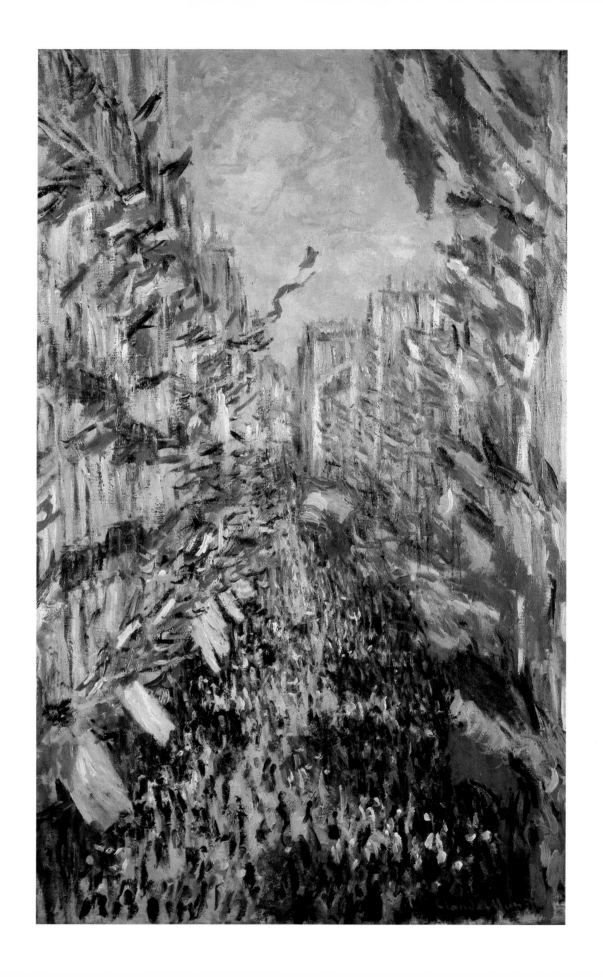

Claude MONET (1840–1926)

L'église de Vétheuil (The Church at Vétheuil), 1879

Oil on canvas, $25\frac{5}{8} \times 19\frac{3}{4}$ (65 × 50)

Gift of Max and Rosy Kaganovitch, 1973 (R.F. 1973–18)

In September 1878, Monet wrote to tell his friend Murer of his recent move to 'Vétheuil, beside the Seine – a really delightful place'. This village, on the right bank of the Seine, was in an unusual situation. Up on a bluff, it overlooked a bend of the river, scattered with wooded islets. It was the kind of landscape which was bound to fascinate the painter, giving him something which was different from Argenteuil, but still near to Paris.

During his first winter at Vétheuil, Monet several times depicted the village under snow. He often chose to take up a position somewhat removed from the scene itself – he would paint it from the river on his boat converted to make a studio, or from one of the islets, or else from the opposite bank. Monet's paintings show the houses with their snowy roofs grouped around the church, a collegiate building of the twelfth century altered during the Renaissance. In the background can be seen the square tower which dominates the composition. It is prominent here because it is seen from a viewpoint somewhat closer than Monet usually chose, and the upright format of the painting stresses the verticality of its architecture which is counterbalanced by the horizontal foreground. In order to render the snowy river bank and the movement of the water, the artist has had recourse to the fragmented touch he had begun to use at Argenteuil. Snow often fascinated Monet and the Impressionists, following in the wake of Courbet, because it prompted a close study of the effects of light and reflection (see also p. 142). This wintry landscape evokes a mood of sadness which can be attributed not only to the season but to the financial and personal preoccupations felt by the artist at this time. This mood characterizes most of the paintings done at Vétheuil, and in particular the series showing the breaking up of the ice, which dates from the winter of 1879–80.   SG-P

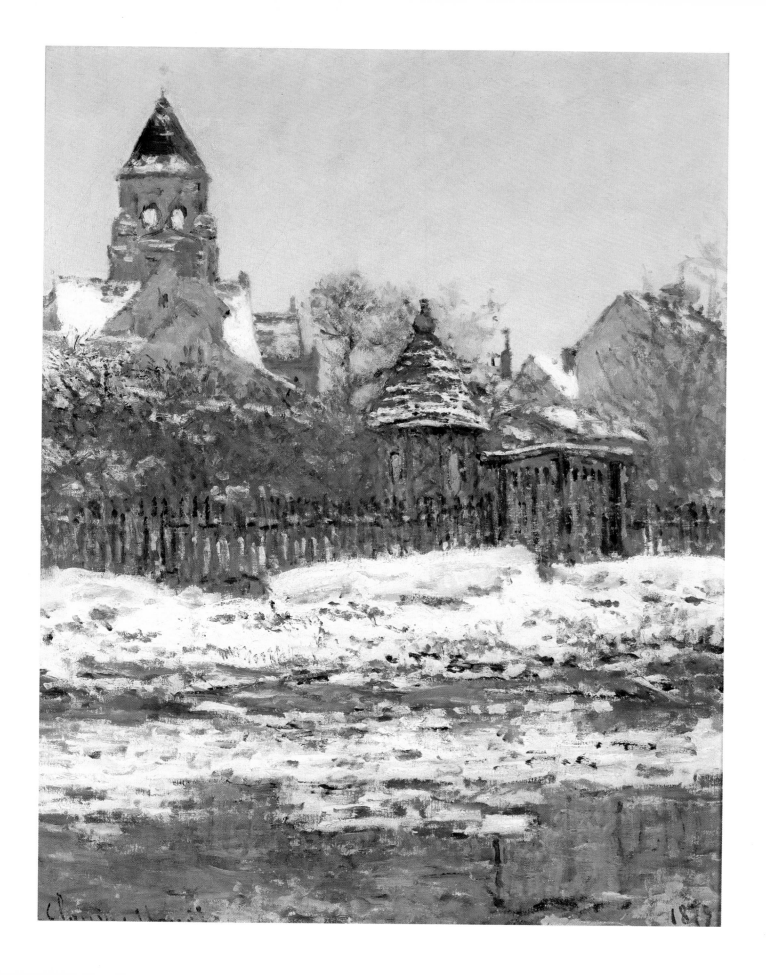

Claude MONET (1840–1926)

Femme à l'ombrelle tournée vers la gauche

(*Woman with a Parasol, Turned Towards the Left*), 1886

Oil on canvas, $51\frac{5}{8} \times 34\frac{5}{8}$ (131 × 88)

Gift of Michel Monet, son of the artist, 1927 (R.F. 2621)

In August 1887, Monet wrote from Giverny to the critic Duret: 'I'm working as hard as ever, but on something new – figures in the open air as I understand them, treated like landscape. It's an old dream which has always plagued me, and I'd like to realize it at last – but it's so difficult!'

The artist had for a long time abandoned figure painting, which he had attempted at the beginning of his career (see p. 88), and also when he was at Argenteuil. Suddenly, around 1885, and for the last time, Monet started to work on the relationship of figures to landscape. He treated the problem from the point of view of an Impressionist landscape painter, concerning himself above all with the light enveloping his characters. His favourite models were the daughters of Alice Hoschedé, whom he was then living with, and who was to become his second wife.

Suzanne Hoschedé, then aged eighteen, must have been the model for the *Femme à l'ombrelle*; the artist shows her walking at Giverny sometime during the summer of 1886. In the pair of paintings given by Monet's son to the Louvre, the painter rendered the moment just as it presented itself to him – clearly it was something which evoked memories of his first wife. In 1875 he had painted Camille in a similar pose, walking along a cliff-top and silhouetted against the sky. Here, in this painting, Monet was so much struck by the impression the scene made on him that he has barely sketched in the face, and has thus depersonalized the model. The two pictures were exhibited at Durand-Ruel's gallery in 1891, under the significant title *Essai de figure en plein air* (*Attempt at Figure-painting in the Open Air*). Monet has tried to render the play of light and shadow produced by the parasol. The movement of the woman's dress and of the plants shows the direction of the wind, and the figure moves in step with the movement of the clouds in the background. SG-P

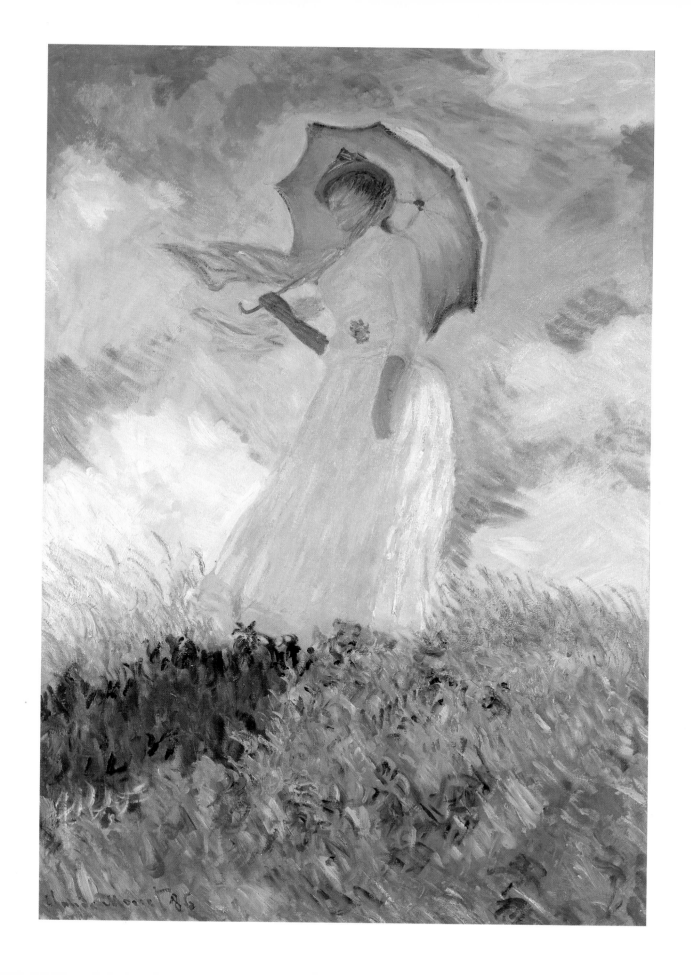

Claude MONET (1840–1926)

La cathédrale de Rouen, le portail, temps gris

(*Rouen Cathedral, the West Portal, Dull Weather*), dated '94', painted 1892

Oil on canvas, $39\frac{3}{8} \times 25\frac{5}{8}$ (100 × 65)

Count Isaac de Camondo bequest, 1911 (R.F. 1999)

La cathédrale de Rouen, le portail et la tour Saint-Romain, plein soleil, harmonie bleue et or

(*Rouen Cathedral, the West Portal and Saint-Romain Tower, Full Sunlight, Harmony in Blue and Gold*), dated '94', painted 1893

Oil on canvas, $42\frac{1}{8} \times 28\frac{3}{4}$ (107 × 73)

Count Isaac de Camondo bequest, 1911 (R.F. 2002)

In the 1890s, Monet's art underwent a decisive change, presaged in work done earlier. It was now only very rarely that the painter tackled a motif in isolation. He worked on several 'series' at sites near his house at Giverny, depicting oat-fields, haystacks and poplars. In these he analysed the variations of light as the hours and seasons passed.

The process of making works in series, on the same theme, was done in an especially systematic way when Monet set up his easel in front of the west façade of Rouen cathedral. Although the pictures are dated 1894, they were done in two sessions in 1892 and 1893 (on each occasion from February to mid-April), from three very slightly different viewpoints. They were then brought to completion in the studio at Giverny.

The many letters he wrote to his wife reveal Monet's method of work and the persistence with which he tackled the subject during his two visits to Rouen. In April 1892 Monet wrote to Alice: 'every day I add something, and catch something by surprise which I hadn't previously been aware of. It's terribly difficult, but things are progressing, and give me a few more days of fine weather and a good number of pictures will be saved. I'm worn out, I can't go on, and yet . . . I had a night full of nightmares: the cathedral was tumbling on top of me – it was all blue and pink and yellow.'

continued on next page

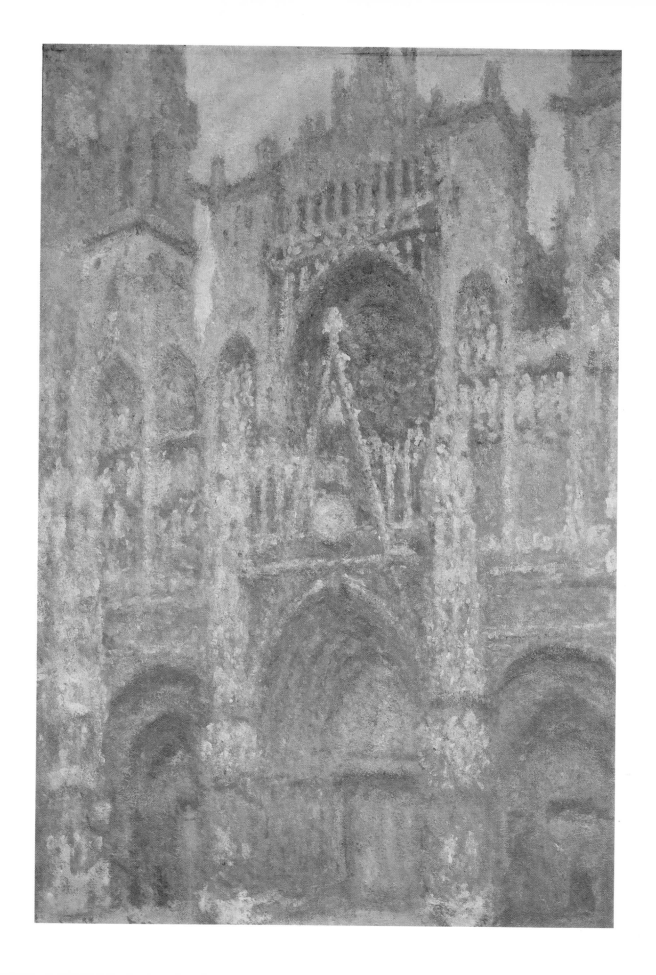

continued from previous page

This series is the most important of all in matter of numbers. There are thirty different versions in which the theme, always identical, is shown from the same point of view – unlike those of haystacks, where the point of view differs. These cathedrals provide the most spectacular demonstration of Monet's determination to catch the instantaneous. The multiplication of canvases corresponds to Monet's sensitivity, which became more and more finely attuned to atmospheric variation with changing weather conditions, and to changes in the light during the course of the day. He directed his attention to the play of light and shadow on the façade of the cathedral. He did not study its architecture for its own sake, but as a support for pictorial researches which aimed to make perceptible the way forms changed in ever-different conditions of lighting. Even a monument as solid and permanent as this one was subject to these transformations. 'Everything alters, even stone', as the artist himself noted in 1893. In order to suggest the physical substance of what he was painting, the painter used a distinctive rough texture to catch the light and give the effect of sunlight moving across stone.

After having several times put off showing the cathedrals, Monet included twenty versions in an exhibition of recent work organized by Durand-Ruel in 1895. The importance and originality of Monet's development was not lost on contemporary painters and writers. Among the eulogies which appeared in the press, the one which touched the artist most was the long article by Georges Clemenceau, in *La Justice* of 20 May 1895, entitled 'Révolution de cathédrales' ('Revolution of Cathedrals'). 'The painter shows us, in twenty canvases, each judiciously different in its effect, the feeling he could have, or would have, experienced in making fifty, or a hundred, or a thousand paintings – as many paintings as there might be moments in his life, if his life was to last as long as this monument made of stone.'

Like Pissarro in his correspondence with his son, Clemenceau stressed the 'lesson' they taught and the unity which could be learned from the whole series, and both of them regretted its imminent dispersal. The presence of five versions, each with a different colour 'harmony', in the Jeu de Paume (one of them bought by the state from Monet in 1907 and the other four forming part of the Camondo bequest) allows us to imagine how the exhibition of 1895 may have looked, when these were shown with the others.   SG-P

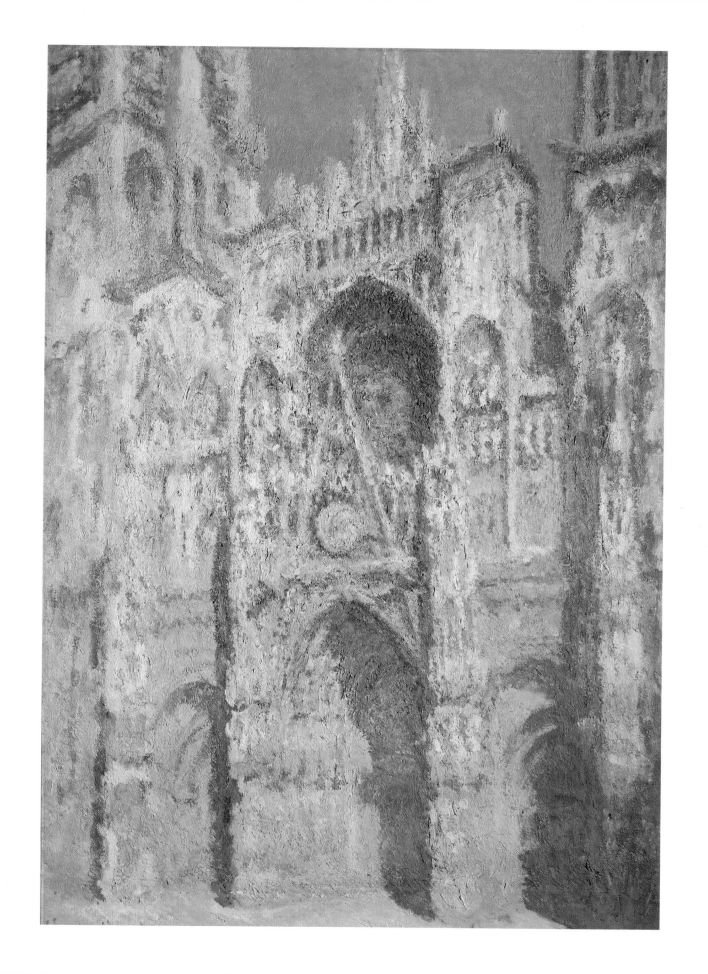

Claude MONET (1840–1926)

Nymphéas bleus (*Blue waterlilies*), nd

Oil on canvas, 78¾ × 78¾ (200 × 200)
Purchased in 1981 (R.F. 1981–40)

In 1893, Monet had the famous waterlily pool made at Giverny. The originality of this water garden, which also reveals the influence of Japanese prints, stems from the fact that it was made entirely to the artist's own design. He thought of it as a painting – something which was stressed by Proust at the beginning of this century.

Monet painted the pool from 1895 onwards, but it was only in 1898 that several works were entirely devoted to it. From 1904 the surrounding landscape and Japanese bridge progressively disappeared and were finally eliminated. The surface of the water itself now occupied the whole canvas. This became the painter's chief subject during the last twenty years of his life. Monet himself wrote to his friend Geffroy in 1908: 'I'm absorbed in work. These landscapes showing water and reflections have become an obsession. I'm an old man, and it's beyond my strength, but I want to represent what I experience.'

The artist made use of the contrasts between the waterlilies and the pond, between the leaves and the flowers, and between the areas which absorbed light and those which reflected it. To give an illusion of unlimited space, the waterlilies are often cut by the edge of the picture. The composition itself is perfectly square – a format very often adopted by Monet at this time. The intense violet colouring is sometimes attributed to changes in the painter's eyesight – he was by this time suffering from eye-trouble.

Monet's researches culminated in the eight large pictures given by him to the state in 1922, and hung in the Orangerie des Tuileries in 1927. With these *Nymphéas*, Monet, the leader of the Impressionists, became a twentieth-century artist – the precursor of abstraction. Ever since he painted them, his 'landscapes in water' have aroused the admiration of painters, writers and musicians.   SG-P

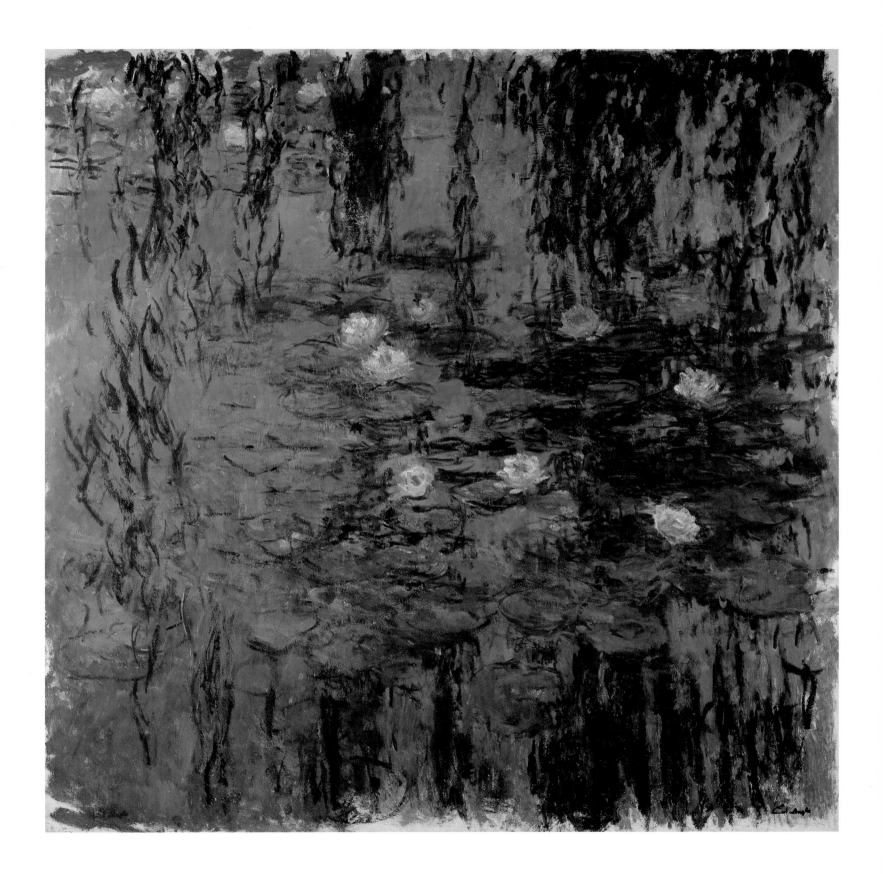

Berthe MORISOT (1841–1895)

Le berceau (*The Cradle*), 1872

Oil on canvas, 22 × 18⅛ (56 × 46)
Purchased in 1930 (R.F. 2849)

Berthe Morisot, the daughter of an important government official, began drawing lessons very early, then from 1861 worked in the open air under the tuition of Corot. Her parents were happy to entertain her artist friends, Degas, Stevens and Fantin-Latour. Through the last she met Manet in 1868, when she was copying paintings by Rubens in the Louvre. Manet gave her advice, and she posed for some of his most striking portraits. (She appears seated in *Le balcon*, p. 82, which was shown at the Salon of 1869.) Later, in 1874, she married Manet's brother Eugène. Despite these links, she did not refuse – as Manet did – to take part in independent exhibitions organized by Renoir, Monet and their friends. She ceased to exhibit at the Salon, and showed her work, from 1874 to 1886, in seven of the eight Impressionist exhibitions, missing that of 1879 only because of the birth of her daughter Julie.

To the exhibition of 1874, at Nadar's studio, where she was the only woman to exhibit, she sent nine works: paintings, pastels and watercolours. The first of her exhibits in the list is *Le berceau*, a miracle of charm and freshness. The model is her sister Edma, now Madame Pontillon – who had studied painting at the same time as Berthe, and who had exhibited at the Salon in 1864 and 1868 – together with her new baby, Blanche. Blanche, a blonde child, can also be recognized, together with her older sister Jeanne, a brunette, in *La chasse aux papillons* (*Chasing Butterflies*, Jeu de Paume), painted at Maurecourt, where Berthe often went to visit, in 1874. Her ambition, as she noted a little later in her grey notebook, was 'limited to a wish to record something of the passing moment', but she knew how to do this – in her landscapes as well as her portraits – with a kind of classicism, a lightness of touch which attracted praise from the critics. GL

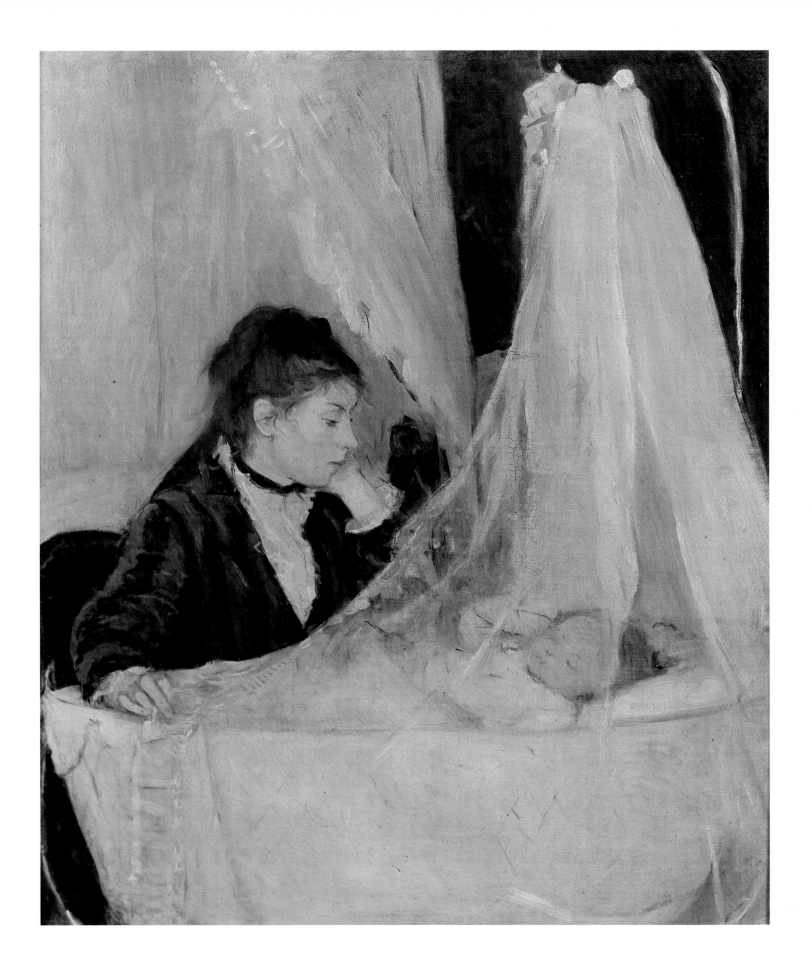

Camille PISSARRO (1830–1903)

Entrée du village de Voisins

(Entrance to the Village of Voisins), 1872

Oil on canvas, $18\frac{1}{8} \times 21\frac{5}{8}$ (46 × 55)

Gift of Ernest May, but retained by him for his lifetime, 1923; entered the Louvre in 1926 (R.F. 2436)

Camille Pissarro was born in St Thomas in the West Indies, then a Danish colony, but most of his career was spent in France, where both his parents came from, and where he settled for good in 1855. By the time he went to London in 1870, and as is most notably demonstrated by some large landscapes shown at the Salon (where Zola admired them), he was in full possession of his artistic powers, and had been responsible for a number of masterpieces. The austere, strongly constructed pictures of this period were certainly those which influenced the early work of Paul Cézanne, who was Pissarro's oldest and most faithful friend. Pissarro's exile to London in 1870 – he took refuge there from the Franco-Prussian War – brought with it a closer relationship with Claude Monet, and was marked by a movement towards a more supple technique and a more colourful palette. When he returned to France, Pissarro, who preferred life in the country to life in Paris, settled first at Louveciennes, then in 1872 went to live at Pontoise, where he remained until 1882. Nearly all the paintings of this period take the landscape of the Ile de France for their subject.

The *Entrée du village de Voisins* is a particularly brightly lit work, and is a good summary of Pissarro's art at this period. He often painted this particular kind of motif – a road bordered with pollarded trees, passing through well-populated countryside, The strongly marked structure of the composition is also a constant in Pissarro's work. The donor of the painting, Ernest May, who was one of the first to collect Impressionist paintings, chose to frame it as a kind of triptych with two other Impressionist landscapes – one by Monet, showing sailing boats at Argenteuil, and the other by Sisley – thus emphasising the particular personality of each artist, while at the same time underlining the similarity of their pictorial experiments.   AD

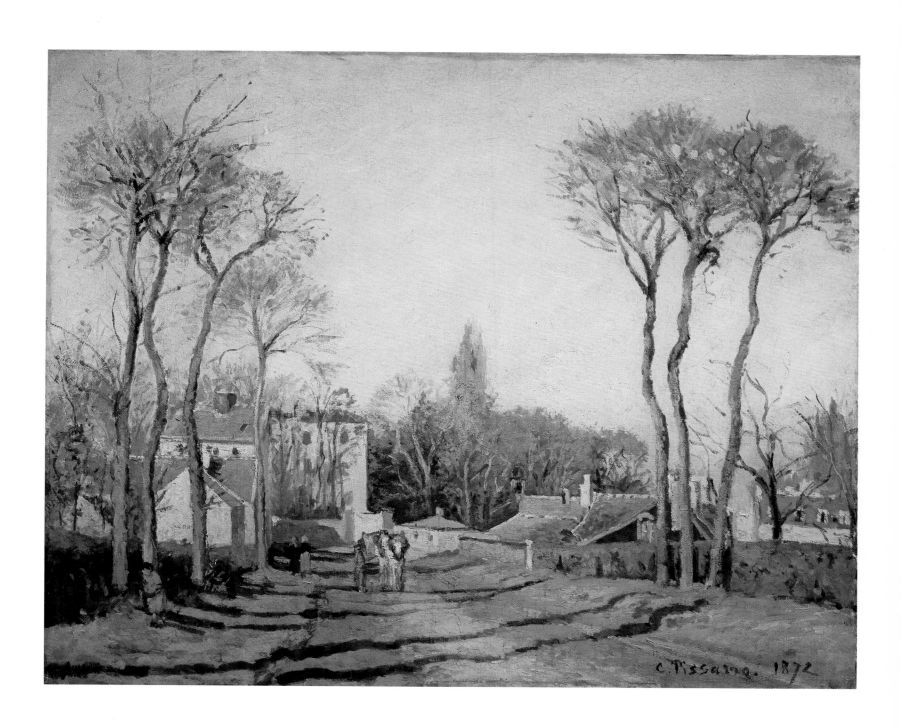

Camille PISSARRO (1830–1903)

Coteau de l'Hermitage, Pontoise (*The Hermitage Hillock, Pontoise*), 1873

Oil on canvas, 24 × 28¾ (61 × 73)

Acquired in lieu of estate duties, 1983 (R.F. 1983–8)

The complex topography of Pontoise, built on an escarpment above the Oise, lent itself to unusual compositions and provided Pissarro with an inexhaustible supply of subject-matter. He particularly liked the intermingling of countryside and town, which can still be seen there today to some extent. In this painting, done with highly fragmented touches of blue, green, grey and beige, the artist uses the contrast between the sinuous lines of the hill and trees and the rectilinear profiles of the buildings. The surprising way the patches of cultivation are handled accentuates still further the bizarre quality of the space thus depicted. As was his custom, Pissarro used the same motif a second time, but painted it under snow. In this, he compares with Monet, who also liked to explore different effects of light on familiar landscapes. When one thinks of this period at Pontoise, it is essential to remember that Paul Cézanne, living sometimes at Pontoise and sometimes in the neighbouring village of Auvers-sur-Oise, often worked side by side with his friend and that such habitual contact set up reciprocal currents of influence.   AD

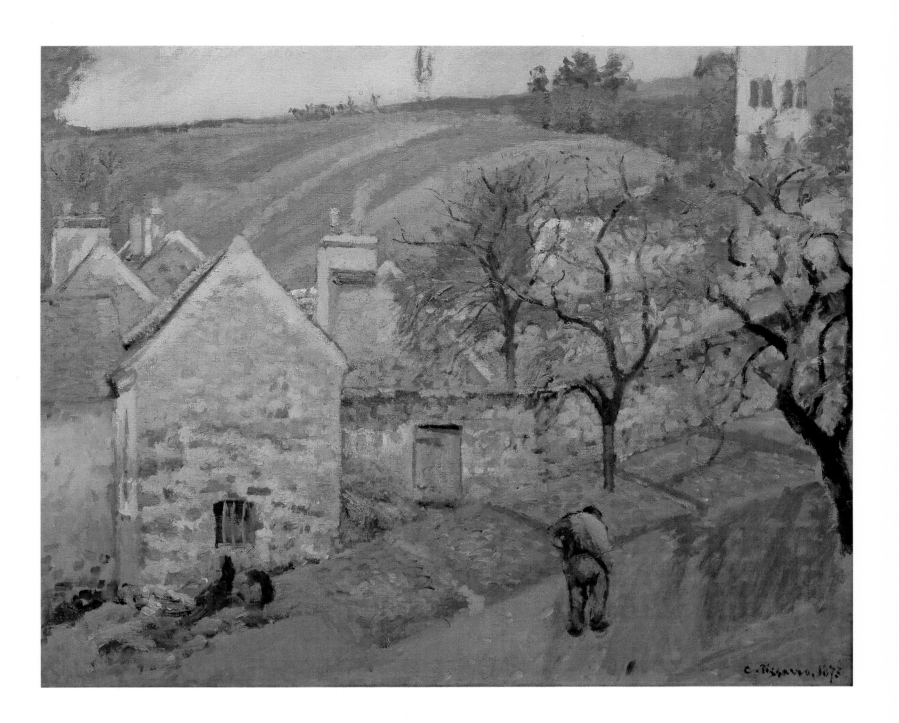

Camille PISSARRO (1830–1903)

Portrait de l'artiste (*Self-portrait*), 1873

Oil on canvas, $22\frac{1}{2} \times 18\frac{1}{8}$ (56 × 46)

Gift of Paul-Emile Pissarro, but retained by him for his lifetime, 1930; entered the Jeu de Paume in 1947 (R.F. 2837)

In 1883, Camille Pissarro wrote to his son Lucien: 'You must remember that I have a rustic, melancholy kind of nature – that there's something unpolished and uncouth about me. People only like me when they've known me for a while – people who take to me have to have a soft spot for me. For the mere passerby a glance is not sufficient – he sees only the surface and, not having the time, he just passes by! ... Painting, and art in general, delight me. They're my whole life. What does anything else matter! ... Isn't that all an artist should really want? Well, that's quite a speech!' This passionate profession of faith accords very well with the extreme simplicity of this self-portrait, where the face alone stands out against a background showing paintings which it is hard to identify, closely hung against a patterned wallpaper of the kind one sees in still-lifes by Pissarro and Cézanne. It is the only self-portrait from this period of his mature work – he did not paint another one until the very end of his life. Pissarro, who was often compared by his contemporaries to Moses, or to God the Father, was soon regarded as a patriarch both because of his physique and because of his kindly nature. The latter, however, did not stop him showing combative energy when it came to organizing the first Impressionist exhibition of 1874, or, later, giving his support to the Anarchist cause, which he did by making drawings to illustrate the periodicals published by the movement. AD

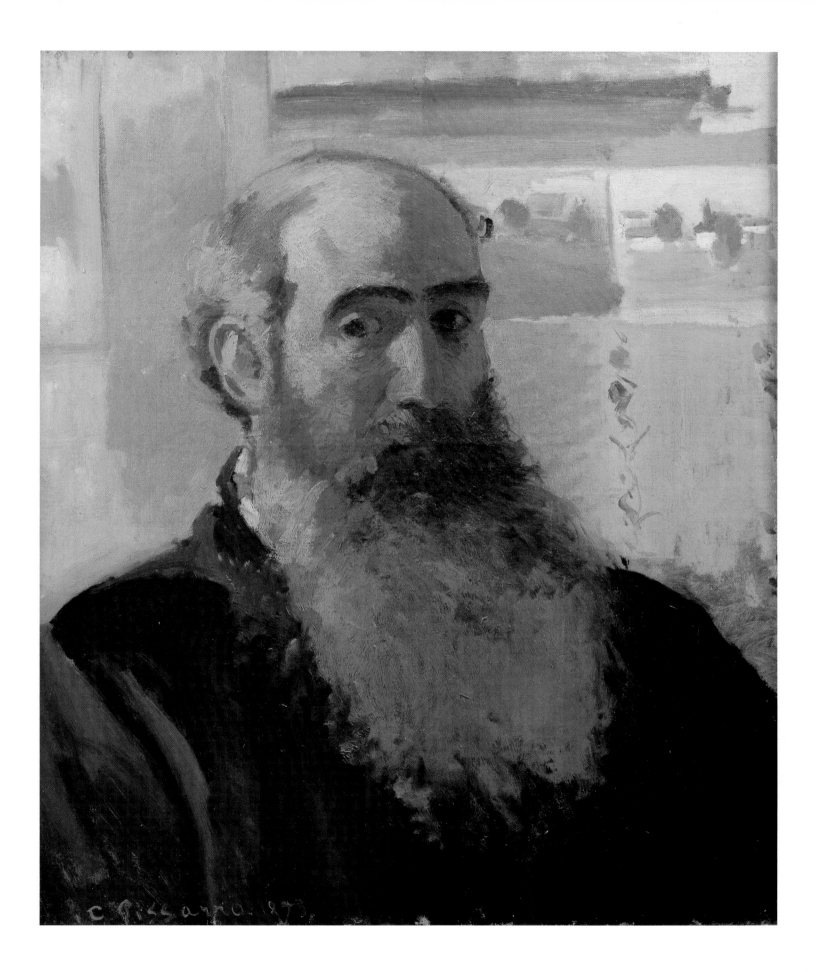

Camille PISSARRO (1830–1903)

Jeune fille à la baguette (*Girl with a Stick*), 1881

Oil on canvas, $31\frac{7}{8} \times 25\frac{1}{4}$ (81×64)

Count Isaac de Camondo bequest, 1911 (R.F. 2103)

For Pissarro, as for the other members of the Impressionist group, the beginning of the 1880s was, if not a time of crisis, then at least one of taking stock of what had happened in the preceding years. *Jeune fille à la baguette* is one of the first paintings in which Pissarro gave such a prominent place to the human figure – with the exception, that is, of self-portraits, the few portraits of members of his family, or of intimate friends such as Cézanne. It is also one of the first where the background has only the kind of importance accorded to the generalized foliage of a 'verdure' tapestry. It is not an isolated work, and can be seen as part of a series of paintings showing young peasant girls in repose. Pissarro's choice of this theme reflects his interest in country people and in their position in contemporary society. It echoes the work of his friend Degas – his 'modern' pictures showing women at work or dancers in rehearsal – rather more than it does that of Millet, to whom Pissarro has often been compared.

The handling – with rough little touches of colour which are sometimes surprisingly bright in hue – calls attention to the sobriety and rigour of the composition. Such figures, often seemingly melancholy, placed in a space which is essentially abstract despite the references to the vegetation which seems actually to support them, particularly stimulated Gauguin, who was then a mere beginner. In fact, it was under Pissarro's aegis that Gauguin painted his first pictures, then exhibited with the Impressionists. AD

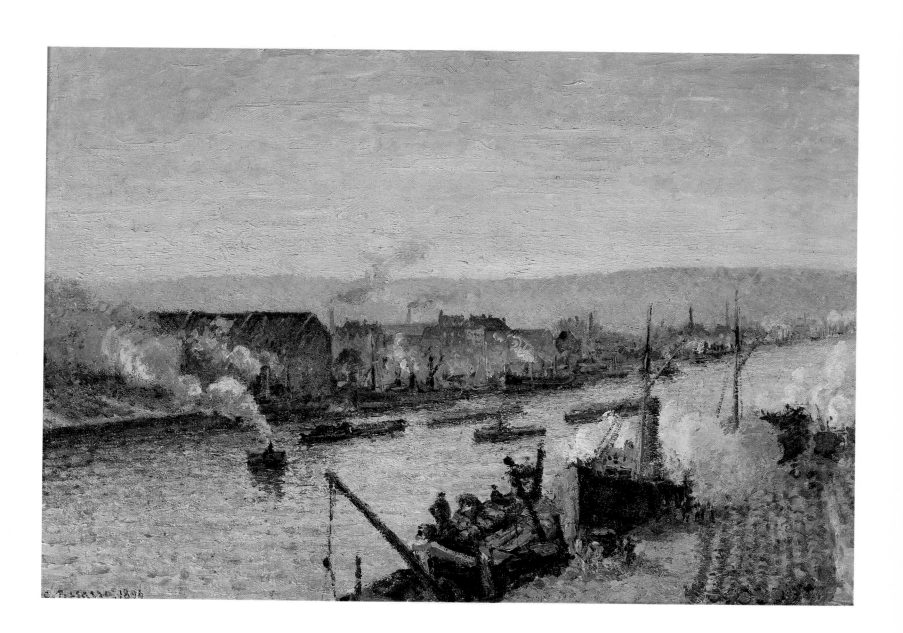

Pierre-Auguste RENOIR (1841–1919)

La liseuse (*Woman Reading*), c. 1874–76

Oil on canvas, 18⅛ × 15 (46 × 38)
Gustave Caillebotte bequest, 1894 (R.F. 3757)

Renoir was born at Limoges, but moved to Paris when he was still very young. His father was a tailor of modest means. Renoir enrolled at the Ecole des Beaux-Arts in 1862, and joined Gleyre's studio, which had the reputation of being the most liberal. There he met Sisley, Bazille and Claude Monet. From 1864 onwards he showed work almost every year at the Salon, with no great success, and in 1874 he took part in the first Impressionist exhibition.

In the 1860s Renoir was strongly influenced by Courbet and by reminiscences of Delacroix. However, he soon created for himself a technique which, although certainly inspired by Manet and Monet, was already strongly individual, supple and fluid. He was above all a figure painter, and had a particular penchant for painting, on a fairly small scale, portraits of women in intimate brightly lit interiors. Women reading, sewing, embroidering – these were the traditional themes which Renoir tackled throughout his career. The model for this particular *Liseuse* is not known, but she can be recognized in other pictures by the artist. Although we do not have the precise information necessary for an exact date, a comparison with the *Moulin de la Galette* (see p. 126), which is more bluish in tone and slightly different in handling, suggests the approximate date of 1874–76.   AD

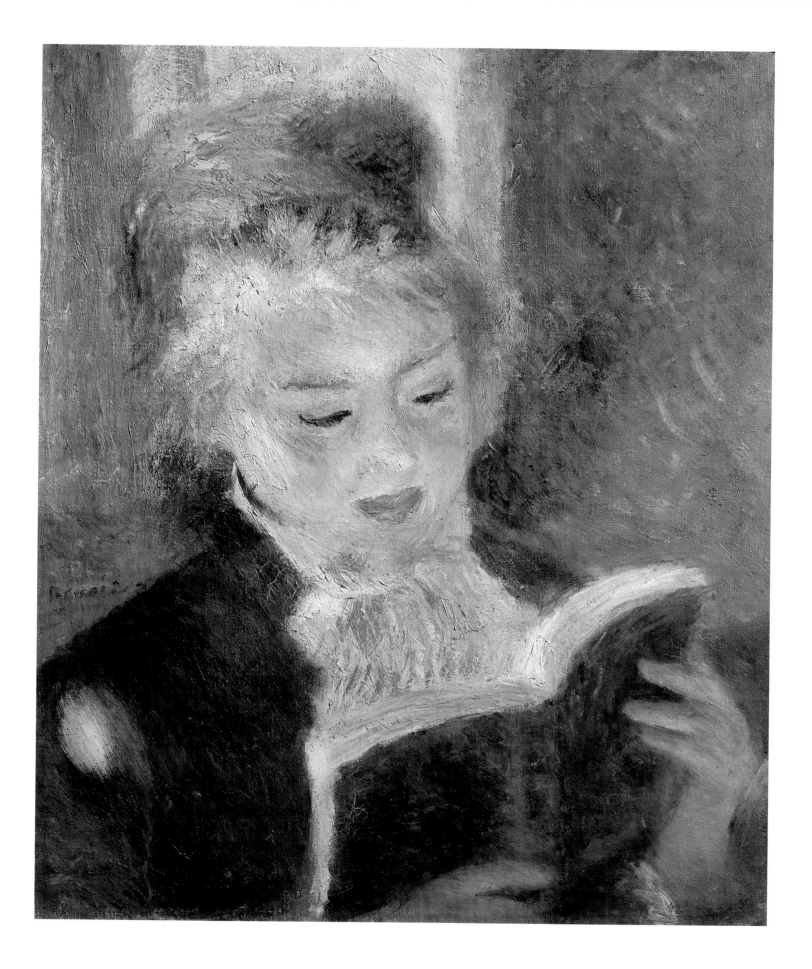

Pierre-Auguste RENOIR (1841–1919)

Le Moulin de la Galette, 1876

Oil on canvas, $51\frac{5}{8} \times 68\frac{7}{8}$ (131×175)

Gustave Caillebotte bequest, 1894 (R.F. 2739)

In 1876, at the time this picture was painted, Montmartre was still a suburb of Paris. Amid gardens and waste land there were several windmills. One of these, the Moulin de la Galette, had given its name to an open-air café, where dances were held on Sundays. At the end of the 1860s Renoir had painted the colourful working-class crowd which frequented the small open-air drinking-places beside the Seine at Chatou. *Bal au Moulin de la Galette*, as this painting was called when it was shown at the third Impressionist exhibition in 1877, uses similar subject-matter as an excuse for representing figures in the open air – a dominant theme in Impressionist painting.

Two sketches for the composition are known – a very cursory one at the Ordrupgaard museum in Copenhagen; a larger and much more finished one in the collection of John Hay Whitney in New York. The latter is actually dated 1876, which has led some people to believe that it is not a sketch but a replica. Renoir's friends posed for the figures, and several of them are identifiable – in the foreground Estelle, seated on a bench; near her Franc-Lamy, the painter Norbert Goeneutte and Georges Rivière, Renoir's future biographer, are grouped round a table covered with glasses. There are other painters among the people dancing; one is the young Gervex, who was to become a member of the Institut National de France. Despite witnesses to the contrary, it is by no means certain that Renoir painted this large canvas entirely on the spot, and it seems probable that it was taken up again and rehandled in the studio, using studies made from life. Although they expressed strong reservations about the work, contemporary critics did understand the artist's intention, and his wish to catch the effect made by light filtering through the leaves and playing on figures which were themselves in movement. The picture entered the national collections with the Caillebotte bequest at a time when Impressionism was still controversial. It soon became famous, and inspired Picasso and Dufy.   AD

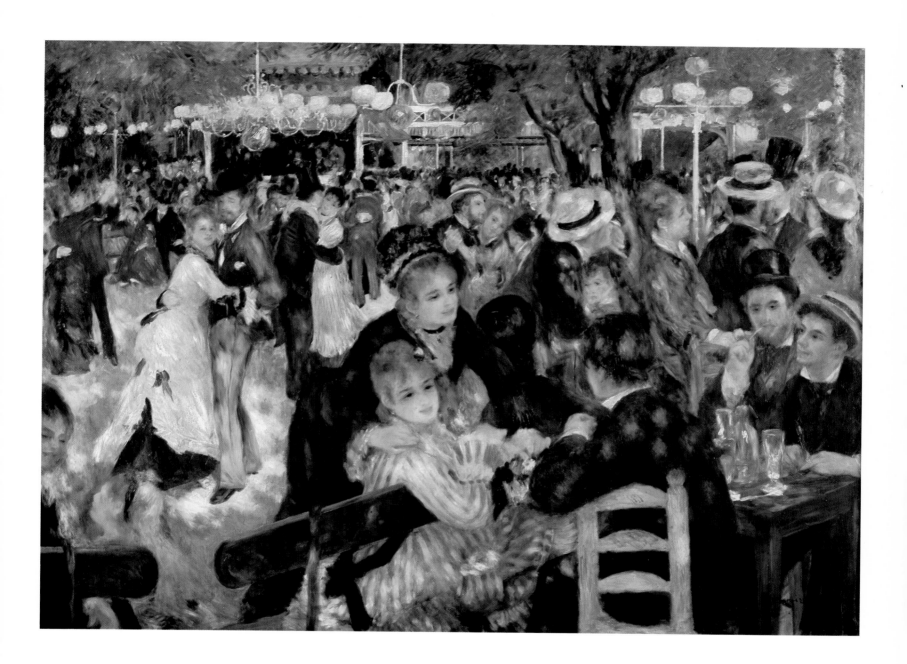

Pierre-Auguste RENOIR (1841–1919)

Chemin montant dans les hautes herbes

(*Path Going up Through Long Grass*), c. 1875

Oil on canvas, $23\frac{5}{8} \times 29\frac{1}{8}$ (60 × 74)

Gift of Charles Comiot through the Friends of the Louvre, 1926 (R.F. 2581)

Renoir's reputation is that of a figure painter, but throughout his career he continued to be interested in landscape. His first landscapes, strongly influenced by Diaz, were painted in the Forest of Fontainebleau, working side by side with friends from Gleyre's studio. His last are of his property near Nice: Les Collettes at Cagnes-sur-Mer. In between, he painted innumerable landscapes in other parts of France – around Paris, in Brittany, in Champagne (particularly at Essoyes, near Troyes, where his wife came from), in Provence and in the Pyrenees. He also found subjects abroad – in Venice, Naples and North Africa.

Although this painting cannot be pinned to a precise spot, there is reason to think that it is a view of a place somewhere near Paris, as it reminds one in many ways of Monet's *Coquelicots* (p. 92). In any case the comparison between these two almost contemporary works is very revealing about the respective styles of the two artists. Monet is bolder and more structured; Renoir plays delightfully with the charm of the unfinished, contrasting passages of silky smoothness with others treated with a thickish impasto.   AD

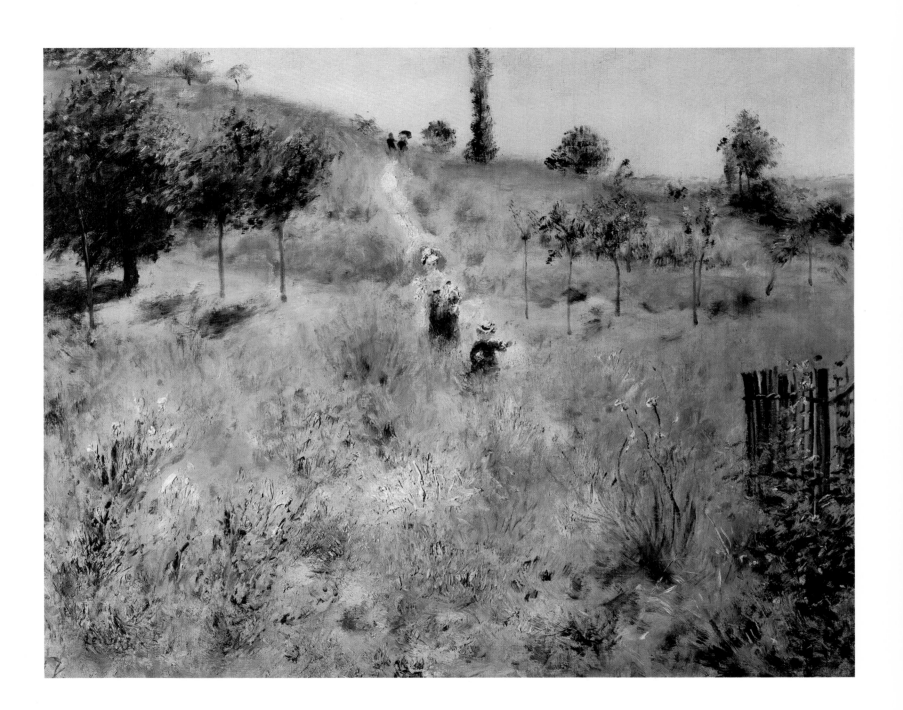

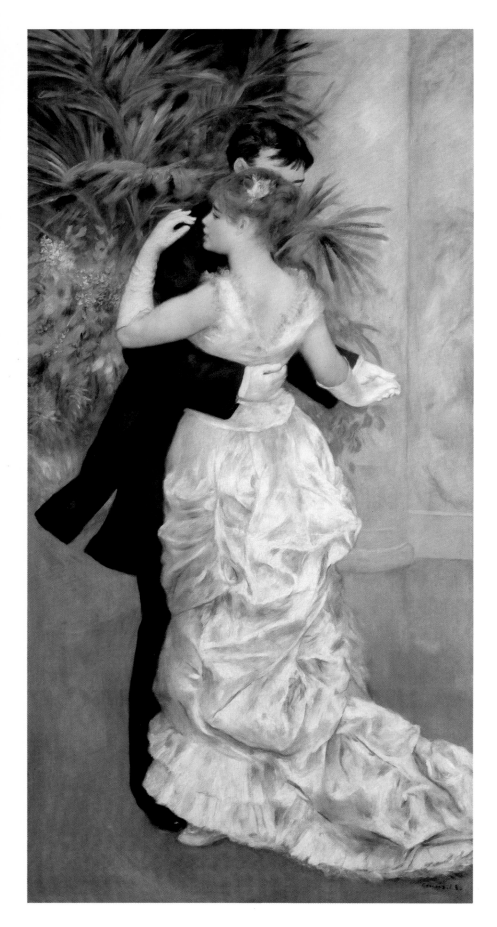

Pierre-Auguste RENOIR (1841–1919)

La danse à la ville
(*The Dance in Town*), 1883

Oil on canvas, $70\frac{7}{8} \times 35\frac{3}{8}$ (180 × 90)
Acquired in lieu of estate duties, 1978 (R.F. 1978–13)

These pictures have been famous since they were shown together at Durand-Ruel's gallery, at Renoir's first one-man show in April 1883 – 'a marvellous exhibition – obviously a great artistic success, for here one can't count on anything else', as Pissarro remarked at the time. They also signal an important new stage in the development of his work. Conceived as a pair, they are in a direct line of descent from *Sisley et sa femme dansant* (*Sisley Dancing with His Wife*, 1868, Wallraf-Richartz Museum, Cologne) and from *Le Moulin de la Galette* (p. 126). The way in which the artist's work was developing in the 1880s is shown by their style; the greater precision of drawing, and the simplification both of form and colour mark a break with the vibrant touch of earlier work. As Renoir himself avowed, the attention he was now paying to draughtsmanship corresponds to the need he felt to renew himself. This was encouraged by a recent trip to Italy, which taught him to appreciate Raphael, and culminated in the great achievement of his *Grandes baigneuses* (*Large Bathers*, Philadelphia Museum of Art).

La danse à la campagne

(The Dance in the Country), 1883

Oil on canvas, 70 × 35 (180 × 90)

Purchased in 1979 (R.F. 1979–64)

The identity of the models has long been the subject of debate, but it seems that Paul Lhôte, a friend of Renoir, posed as the man; in *La danse à la ville* the young woman dancing with him is Suzanne Valadon (herself a painter, as well as being Utrillo's mother), and in *La danse à la campagne* the model is his wife Aline.

The large painting in the Boston Museum of Fine Arts called *Le bal à Bougival*, also painted in 1883, is close to the composition of *La danse à la campagne*, but reversed left to right. AD

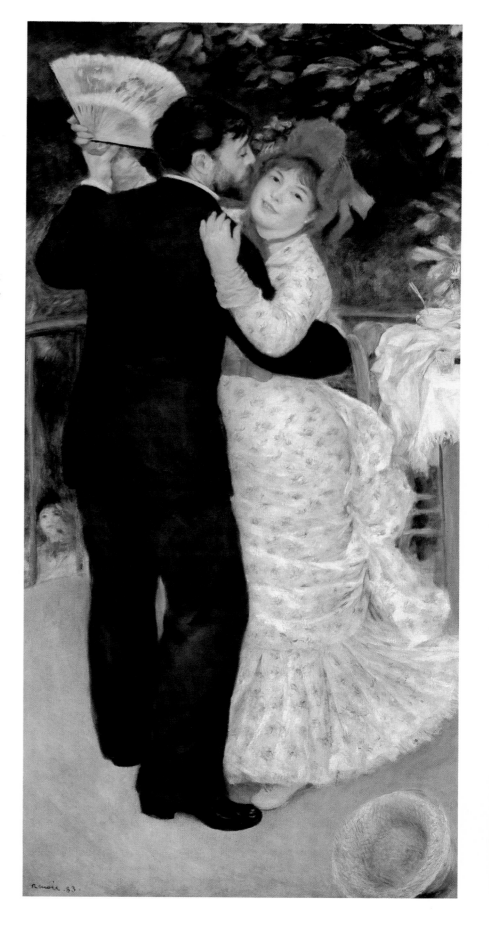

Pierre-Auguste RENOIR (1841–1919)

Jeunes filles au piano (Girls at the Piano), 1892

Oil on canvas, $45\frac{5}{8} \times 35\frac{3}{8}$ (116 × 90)

Purchased in 1892 (R.F. 755)

In the 1880s Renoir was attentive to line and draughtsmanship, and adopted an unexpected palette of cold but bright tones. With *Jeunes filles au piano*, painted in 1892, he is returning to a suppler conception. Nevertheless this painting, with its acidulated colour, demonstrates his concern for compositional balance and for precise modelling – note the hands of the young pianist for instance – something far removed from *Le Moulin de la Galette* (see p. 126).

Renoir loved music, and several times painted girls playing the piano. Some of his pictures on this theme are in fact portraits. But it is not known who posed for this painting in the Jeu de Paume, or for other versions of this composition elsewhere (one in the Lehman Collection in the Metropolitan Museum, New York; one in the Niarchos Collection; a third which once belonged to Gustave Caillebotte; and another very sketchy version in the Walter Guillaume Collection). These girls at the piano are the quintessence of the physical type Renoir preferred, and are in perfect harmony with the cosy bourgeois interior which encloses them like a kind of jewel-case. The whole composition encapsulates perfectly one stage in the evolution of Renoir's painting.   AD

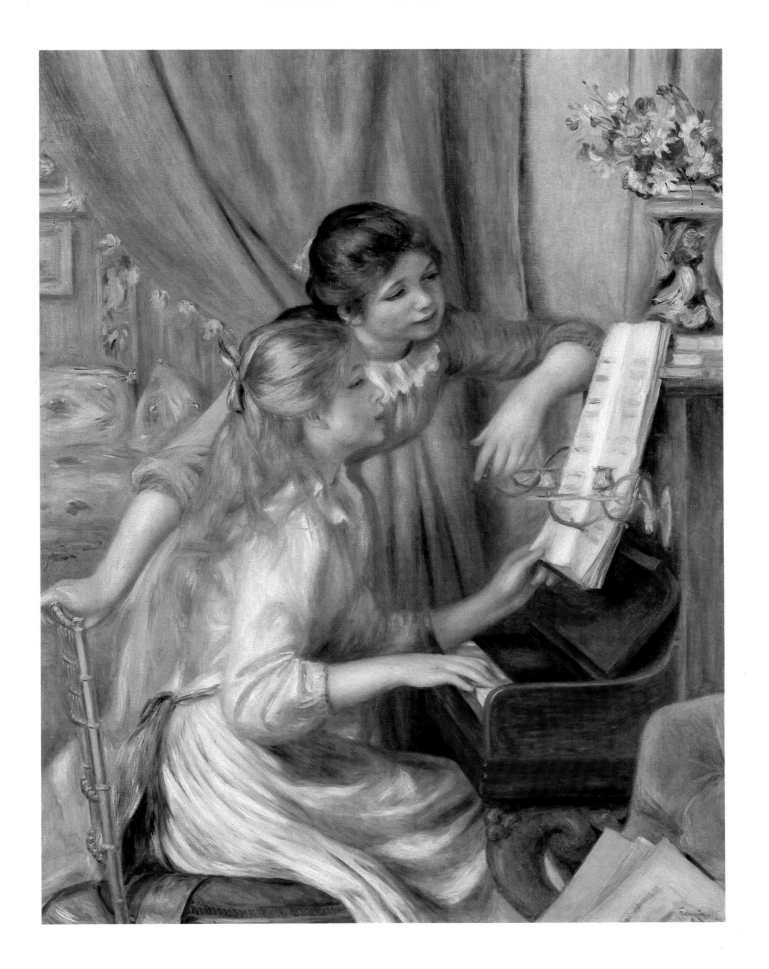

Pierre-Auguste RENOIR (1841–1919)

Les baigneuses (*The Bathers*), 1918

Oil on canvas, 43 × 62½ (110 × 160)
Gift of the artist's sons, 1923 (R.F. 2795)

After 1900, Renoir spent most of his time at his country property Les Collettes, at Cagnes-sur-Mer, near Nice. Crippled with rheumatism and confined to a wheel-chair, he still continued to paint with furious determination. At this time, he amused himself by producing numerous rough sketches which create in a few strokes the profile of a model, the silhouette of a tree or the roundness of an apple. This intimate and carefree production has since become a staple in a certain part of the art-trade, and has made people forget a handful of large compositions – the masterpieces of Renoir's final period, which is also the one least understood by the public.

The female nude was from the beginning of Renoir's career a favourite theme, and, at the end, took on a new importance. He applied the colour-range of dominant red-brown or rosy pink, set off by bright yellows, greens and blues, both to interior scenes and, as here, to a lyrical evocation of the Mediterranean ambience of which the ageing artist had become so fond. These *Baigneuses* immediately call to mind Rubens' great nudes, transported to the luxuriant gardens of the Midi. This reference to the classical tradition does not, however, diminish the audaciousness of the conception of this painting – one which seems intended as Renoir's artistic testament.   AD

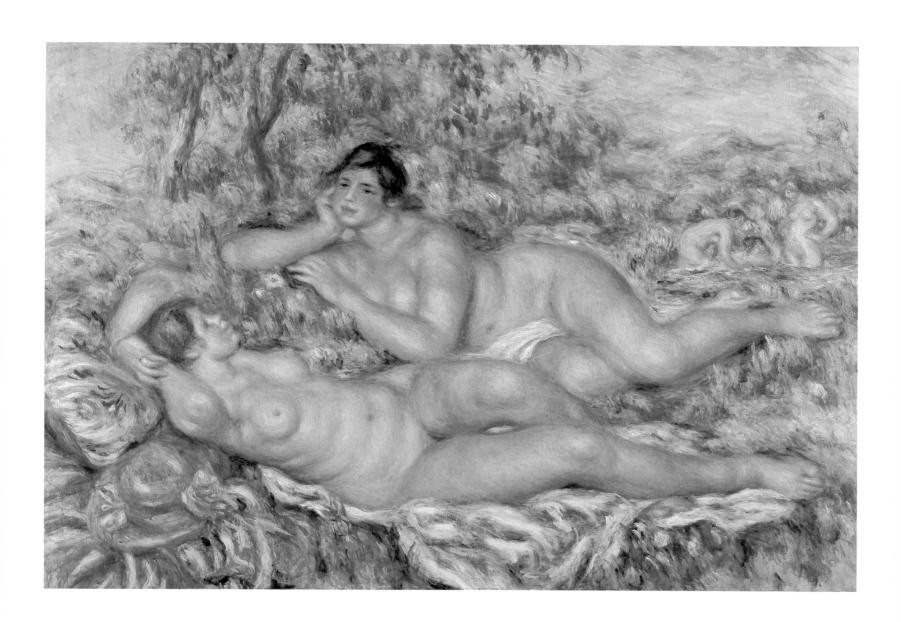

Alfred SISLEY (1839–1899)

Le Chemin de la Machine à Louveciennes, or *La route, vue du chemin de Sèvres*

(The Chemin de la Machine at Louveciennes, or *The Road to Sèvres),* 1873

Oil on canvas, $21\frac{1}{4} \times 28\frac{3}{4}$ (54 × 73)

Gift of Joanny Peytel, but retained by him for his lifetime, 1914; retention abandoned, 1918 (R.F. 2079)

The thing which Sisley strived for in his landscapes was a certain kind of spatial organization. His feeling for construction, probably inherited from Corot, led him to respect the relationship between one plane and another. Thus a road losing itself at the horizon was one of his favourite themes, and recurs frequently in his work. Often it is used to link the foreground to what lies in the distance, helping the eye to 'discover' the space, and contributes to sophisticated effects of perspective.

This three-dimensional illusion is particularly striking when the road recedes at right angles to the picture-plane. To accentuate the effect of depth, the artist has here risked some daring foreshortening in his painting of the trees beside the road. He establishes an interplay of lines between the verticals of the tree-trunks and the horizontals of their shadows. Sisley often took care to humanize his landscapes by putting in some small figures, in the manner of Jongkind. Here he has judiciously used the fact that the road is going slightly uphill to create a vanishing-point which is slightly off-centre, and to provide a view down into the sun-filled distance. (It is now thought that the painting represents the Chemin de la Machine at Louveciennes rather than the Rue de Sèvres, by which title it was formerly known.)

Sisley devoted much study to Corot and to the Barbizon School, and also to landscapes by Dutch seventeenth-century masters. No doubt he discovered, during the period he spent in London when he was young, Hobbema's famous *Avenue at Middleharnis.* And following the example of Ruysdael, who gave a predominant place to the sky, Sisley here accords it considerable importance.

Sisley never managed to obtain French nationality, but has here succeeded wonderfully in rendering the quality of light of the Ile-de-France. The picture certainly was worthy of the honour of being chosen to commemorate Sisley in the Centennial Exhibition of French Art held in connection with the International Exhibition of 1900.   SG-P

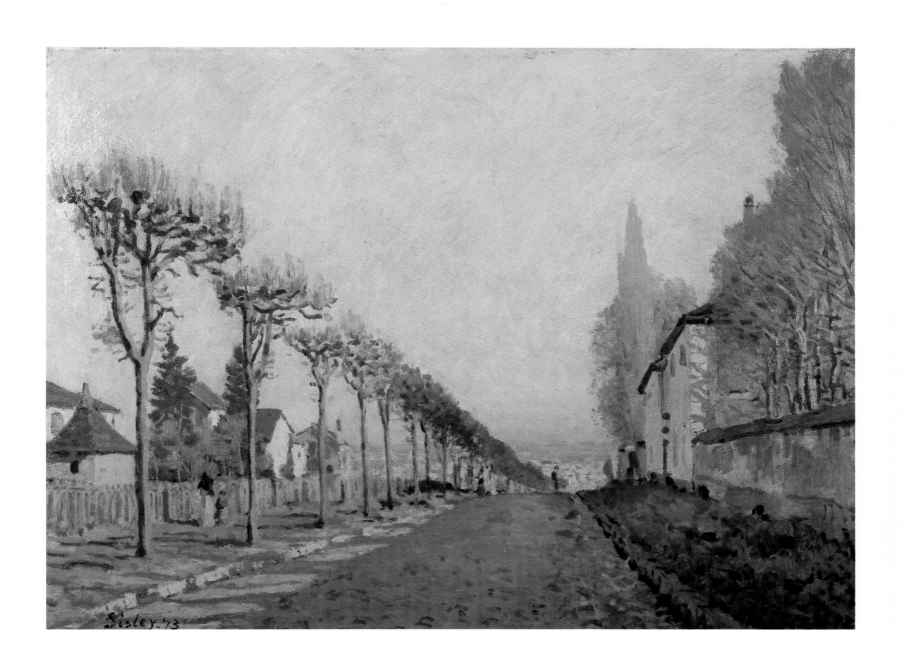

Alfred SISLEY (1839–1899)

Le brouillard, Voisins (*Mist at Voisins*), 1874

Oil on canvas, $19\frac{3}{4} \times 25\frac{5}{8}$ (50 × 65)

Antonin Personnaz bequest, 1937 (R.F. 1937–64)

Sisley had lived at Voisins since 1871. In 1872, Pissarro painted his *Entrée du village de Voisins* (part of the Ernest May triptych, see p. 112). Now Sisley also wanted to paint some views of this little village in what used to be the *département* of Seine-et-Oise, near Louveciennes.

Voisins is probably the spot where he captured this effect of mist. To the left can be seen a group of trees, and in the background a fence enclosing a garden. Under a tree with twisted branches, a woman bends to pick some flowers. The large flowering thickets in the foreground suggest that it is springtime. 'All this is seen through a silvery mist which blurs the forms and gives a grey-blue tonality to the whole', wrote Germain Bazin, suggesting that one can 'perhaps compare the picture with Corot's mysterious early morning scenes.'

'Which painters do I love? To speak only of contemporary artists, our masters Delacroix, Corot, Millet, Rousseau, Courbet. All those who have loved nature and who have felt a close sympathy with it . . .', confided Sisley to the art-critic Adolphe Tavernier in 1892. The artist thus linked himself to the great names of the French school of the nineteenth century; he saw himself as a successor of the Barbizon painters who had abandoned the traditional, classical principles of the artificially composed historical landscape, and who also rejected the picturesque aspect of romantic landscape in favour of a vision closer to nature. This rejection of academic convention can be felt in this work, which is comparable to Monet's 'impressions' and very different from the kind of painting appreciated at the Salon. Sisley did nevertheless show there in 1866, 1868 and 1878 – but this picture dates from 1874, the year of the first Impressionist exhibition in Nadar's studio, in which the artist was represented by five pictures. SG-P

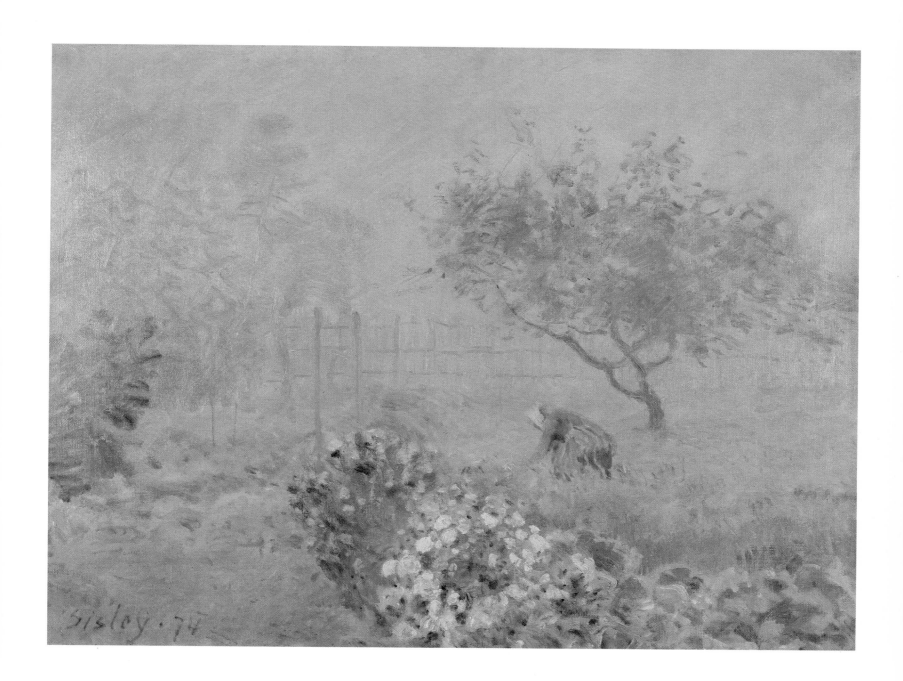

Alfred SISLEY (1839–1899)

L'inondation à Port-Marly (*The Flood at Port-Marly*), 1876

Oil on canvas, $23\frac{5}{8} \times 31\frac{7}{8}$ (60 × 81)

Count Isaac de Camondo bequest, 1911 (R.F. 2020)

The most celebrated of the paintings done by Sisley during his period at Marly-le-Roi (1874–77) are probably those which immortalized the nearby village of Port-Marly, on the banks of the Seine, when it was flooded.

The artist had been interested in this theme from 1872, but it was above all in 1876 that he was able to treat it fully, in a group of six pictures. The best known of these is the large *Inondation à Port-Marly* left to the Louvre by Count Isaac de Camondo. The dominant hues are the grey-blue tints of the sky reflected in the water and interrupted by the more positive colours of the building painted in three horizontal bands. These, with the red of the flag, bring a note of gaiety into the composition. The curtains in the windows recall that the scene would normally have been inhabited; here little black silhouettes, figures whom the artist seems to have borrowed from Jongkind, animate a kind of landscape whose serenity is quite different from the dramatic conception of nature which was dear to the Romantics.

Another picture, also part of the Camondo Collection, *La barque pendant l'inondation* (*The Boat during the Flood*), is smaller, and the artist has adopted a slightly different point of view. It may have been, as P. Jamot says, the 'first thought for the definitive composition'.

In 1880, Monet represented ice being broken on the Seine at Vétheuil in a series of works of a much more dramatic quality than this one. Both painters were attracted by a fleeting and unusual event which allowed them to make a special study of light and of reflections in the river, as well as of the fusion of trees, sky and water. But, although Sisley was influenced at this time by Monet, he differs from his friend in his interest in pictorial construction which leads him to respect the structure of the forms.

This picture appeared at the sale of the critic Tavernier's collection in 1900, barely a year after the artist's death, and was the first work by him to fetch a high price.   SG-P

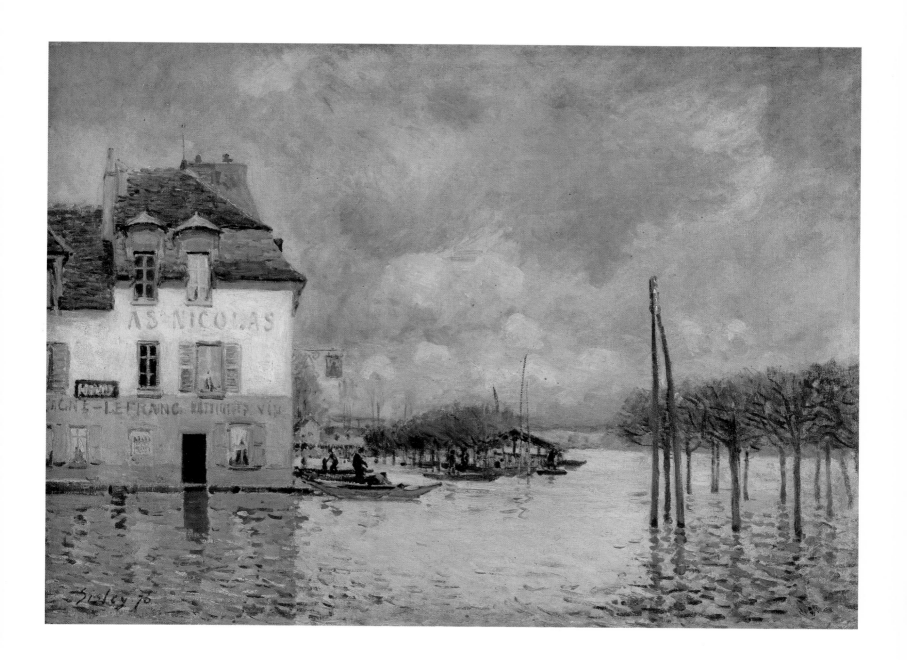

Alfred SISLEY (1839–1899)

La neige à Louveciennes (*Snow at Louveciennes*), 1878

Oil on canvas, 24 × 19⅝ (61 × 50)

Count Isaac de Camondo bequest, 1911 (R.F. 2022)

Sisley was especially attracted by the countryside in winter. His reserved and solitary temperament preferred its mystery and silence to the brilliance of the sunny Mediterranean landscapes associated with Renoir. He excelled at rendering nature's sadness and desolation. Like Monet at the same period (see p. 100), Sisley followed in Courbet's footsteps in painting landscapes under snow. This theme was particularly attractive to the Impressionists because it allowed them to study variations of light in a particular way, and enabled them to use different nuances of the palette and cover the picture with minute touches of colour. Thanks to this fragmentation of brushstrokes, the ground is not uniformly white, but is iridescent with bluish reflections.

The winters Sisley spent at Louveciennes, Marly-le-Roi and Veneux-Nadon inspired him to paint numerous snow-scenes. This one also illustrates the painter's study of perspective; a road covered with snow leads the eye into the picture space, and the little figure at the centre of the composition seems exceptionally isolated in the midst of the wintry countryside. The sensitivity of the artist, which is expressed in these refined and delicate landscapes with their quiet colour harmonies, can perhaps be explained by the fact that he was by birth English. He had also been able to study the work of Bonington, Constable and Turner during four years spent in England between 1857 and 1861, and during later visits there. It is worth remembering that the practice of working in watercolour – very much in favour in England at this time – had given English painting a new freedom of handling.

Sisley's views of Louveciennes under snow were much admired by the famous playwright Georges Feydeau, who owned two different versions. This one was bought by Count Isaac de Camondo at the second Feydeau sale, on 4 April 1903. SG-P

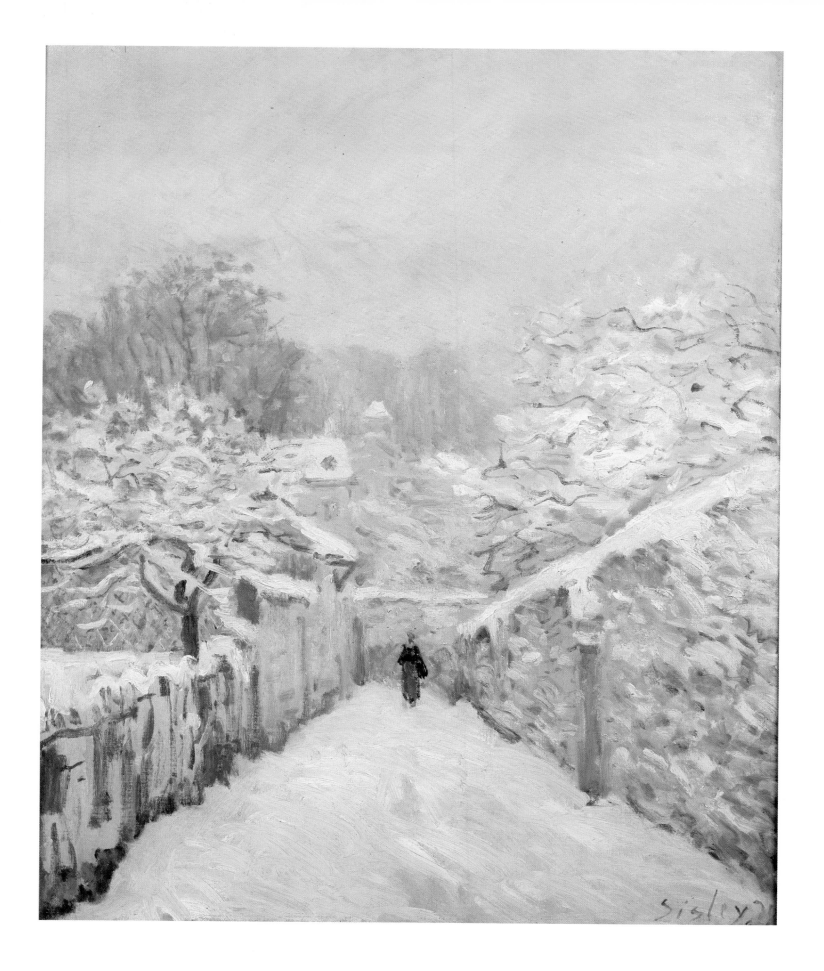

Alfred SISLEY (1839–1899)

Le canal du Loing (*The Loing Canal*), 1892

Oil on canvas, $28\frac{3}{4} \times 36\frac{5}{8}$ (73 × 93)

Given to the Musée du Luxembourg by a group of the artist's friends, 1899 (INV. 20 723)

In 1880 there was a great change both in Sisley's life and in his work; the painter left the *département* of Seine-et-Oise where he had lived and worked since 1871, and took up residence in Seine-et-Marne, where he lived until his death nineteen years later. First, he settled south of Fontainebleau, at Veneux-Nadon; then in September 1882 he went to Moret-sur-Loing, which he left in 1883 for Les Sablons. In November 1889 he returned to Moret-sur-Loing for good; his choice is not surprising, as it was a picturesque little town, with a charming position beside the river Loing.

In the last twenty years of his life, Sisley often painted views beside the Loing, or on the Seine at Saint-Mammès, where the Loing runs into the Seine. On 7 March 1884, Sisley wrote to Durand-Ruel: 'I've started work again, and I have several pictures on the go (views beside the river)'.

This, one of Sisley's numerous paintings of the Loing Canal, came to the Luxembourg in 1899, as the gift of a group of the artist's friends organized for the purpose by Monet. The structure of the composition is original. The painter chose a spot where the canal was just entering a bend and from which he could see the opposite bank through a screen of poplars with bare trunks. His way of tackling the motif recalls the perspective effects he had created previously with views of roads turning and then losing themselves on the horizon.

In the same year that this picture was painted, Sisley gave the following explanation of his art to the critic Tavernier: 'The sky cannot be merely a background . . . I stress this element in landscape painting because I'd like to get you to understand the kind of importance I attach to it . . . When I start a painting, I always start with the sky.'   SG-P

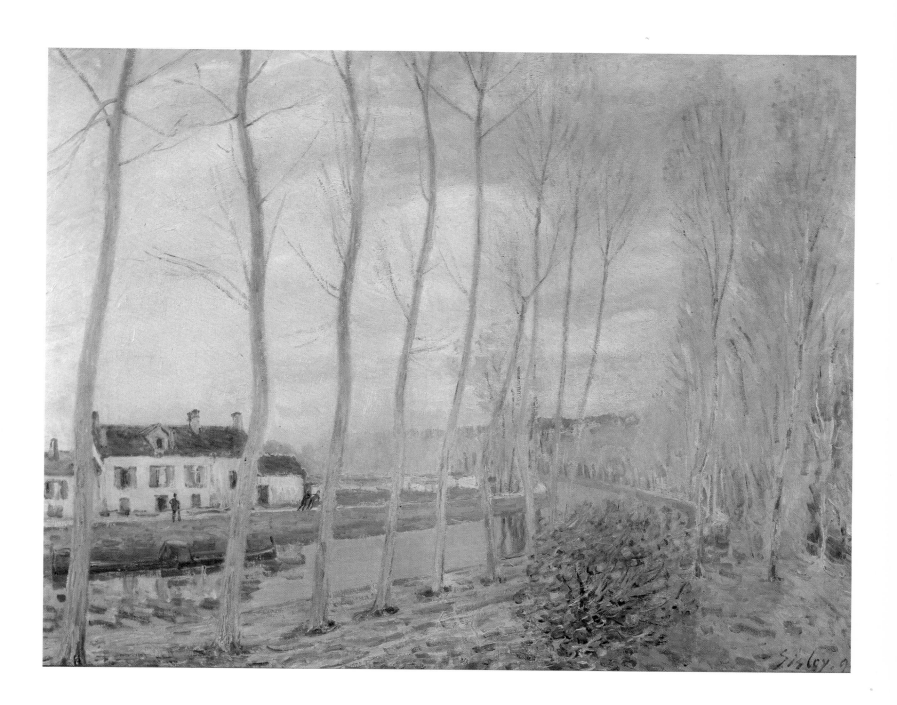

Vincent VAN GOGH (1853–1890)

L'Italienne (*The Italian Woman*), 1887

Oil on canvas, $31\frac{7}{8} \times 23\frac{5}{8}$ (81 × 60)

Gift of Baroness Eva Gebhard-Gourgaud, 1965 (R.F. 1965–14)

Van Gogh, son of a Dutch pastor, only discovered his vocation as a painter in 1880, when he was twenty-seven. Before that there had been a time of drifting during which, uncertain of his vocation, he studied theology, then worked for the picture-dealer Goupil at The Hague, in London, and finally in Paris. His discovery of what he wanted to do was followed by a series of dark pictures, with thick impasto; typical of these is the *Tête de paysanne hollandaise* (*Head of a Dutch Peasant Woman*) of 1884, in the Jeu de Paume. Very different are the paintings which Van Gogh painted in Paris, after he came there to live with his brother Theo in 1886. *L'Italienne* is a dazzling example. The artistic milieu which Van Gogh then discovered was in a state of full effervescence, and he came into contact with avant-garde artists like Toulouse-Lautrec and Emile Bernard. He was at once able to make use of the innovations introduced by Impressionism, whose status was now confirmed. The immediate effect was to convert him to colour – his palette needed only to be unleashed in its full force – as can be seen in *La guinguette* (*The Open-air Tavern*) of 1886, and in *Le Restaurant de la Sirène* of 1887.

The sitter for *L'Italienne*, in her brilliant costume, was in all probability Agostina Segatori, the owner of a Paris cabaret called Le Tambourin. She was well known in the world of painters, particularly as one of Manet's former models. Her establishment, where Van Gogh hung his own paintings and some of his Japanese prints, was frequented by artists and writers – among them Steinlen, Forain, Bonnard and Gauguin. The severe design of the picture, which is almost abstract with its monochrome yellow background and rigid edging striped with red and green, is derived from Japanese models. It is vigorously painted, with a nervous brush-stroke which gives the whole composition a dazzling chromatic vibration. Taking a hint from Seurat, Van Gogh made use of complementary colours, arbitrarily employed, and thus shows himself to be a precursor of Fauvism, and of the expressionist and abstractionist art movements which followed.   CF-T

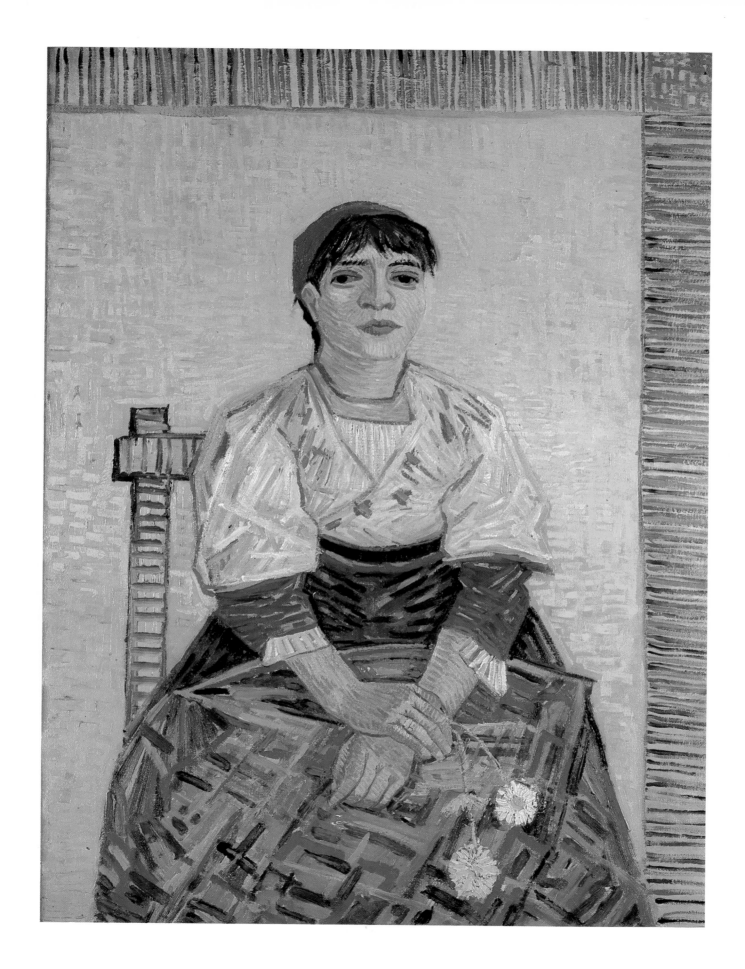

Vincent VAN GOGH (1853–1890)

La salle de danse à Arles (The Dance-hall at Arles), 1888

Oil on canvas, $25\frac{5}{8} \times 31\frac{7}{8}$ (65 × 81)

Gift of M. and Mme André Mayer, but retained by them for their lifetime, 1950; retention abandoned, 1975 (R.F 1950–9)

Van Gogh fled from Paris to the Midi, and arrived at Arles in February 1888. Dazzled by the southern light, he proceeded to paint some of his best-known works, for example *Les Tournesols* (*The Sunflowers*), *Le facteur Roulin* (*Roulin the Postman*) and *L'Arlésienne* (*Woman of Arles*); this last can also be seen at the Jeu de Paume. No sooner had he got to Arles than Van Gogh began to try to get Gauguin to come there too – for Gauguin completely fascinated him. *La salle de danse à Arles* is without any doubt the painting where Gauguin's influence over Van Gogh is most visible, and, through Gauguin, also that of his young disciple at Pont-Aven, Emile Bernard. Gauguin had in fact brought with him a surprising painting by Bernard of *Bretonnes dans une prairie verte* (*Breton Women in a Green Meadow*) in an extremely synthetist style, much removed from any kind of realism and in which the figures of the peasant women were encircled by harsh black lines and appeared against a raw green background. Van Gogh made a copy of this picture and borrowed several technical devices from it in *La salle de danse* – for example, the outlines of the forms; bold, flatly painted colours as opposed to the broken touch of the Impressionists; and the irregular silhouettes of the women in the foreground. What we have here is a semi-experimental work in which Van Gogh is trying to get to the bottom of a pictorial theory which is verging on abstraction. But his fiery temperament imbues the picture with a kind of frenzy in which the faces are pushed to the brink of caricature. It is nevertheless possible to identify Madame Roulin, wife of Van Gogh's friend the postman, on the right; the painter has immortalized them both in the individual portraits he painted of them. At exactly the same period Seurat and Lautrec were both using this kind of subject-matter – night-scenes done in popular dance-halls – as the basis for works which were radically new.   CF-T

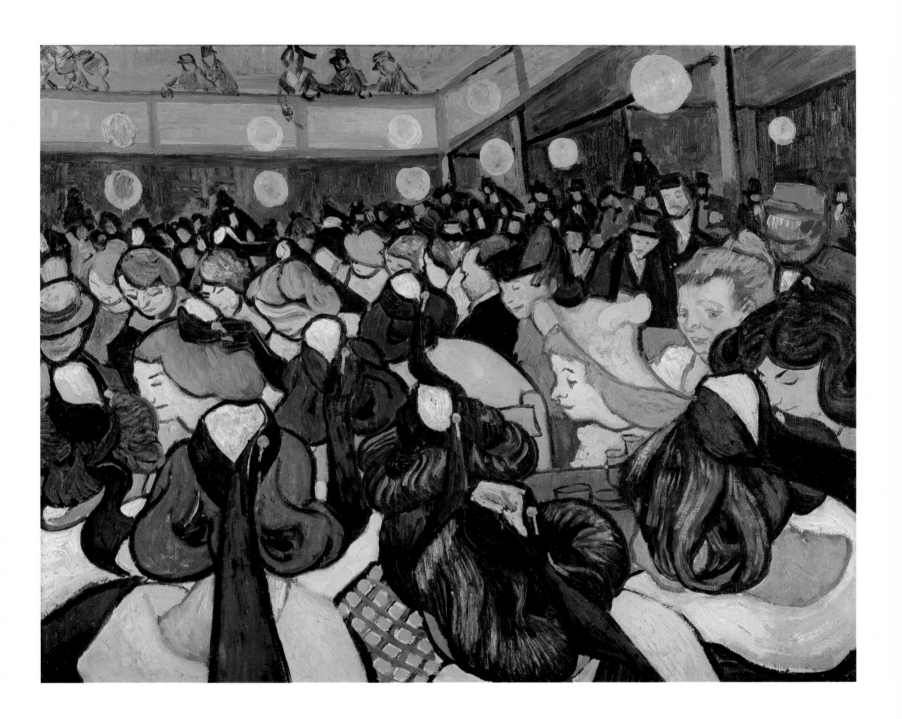

Vincent VAN GOGH (1853–1890)

Portrait de l'artiste (*Self-portrait*), 1889

Oil on canvas, $25\frac{5}{8} \times 17\frac{3}{4}$ (65 × 45)

Gift of Paul and Marguerite Gachet, 1949 (R.F. 1949–17)

This moving self-portrait is one of the last in a long series. There are about forty of them, in oils, done by an artist obsessed with the idea of confronting his own image. There can be nothing astonishing about the fact that this man – who was mentally unstable and subject to frequent and violent nervous crises – should have tried to exorcize his demons by projecting them into art. He is the precursor here of a succession of Expressionist artists, such as Munch, Ensor, Jawlensky and Kokoschka, all of whom frequently turned to the self-portrait.

Van Gogh is simultaneously the classic instance of the *artiste maudit* ('accursed artist') – an idea often put forward and widely accepted during the nineteenth century – and one of the founding fathers of our own conception of the modern: this is something which readily explains the immense popular success of the self-portrait and others such as the famous *Autoportrait à l'oreille coupée* (*Self-portrait with Severed Ear*), or the example showing Van Gogh in a straw hat. In this picture, which, according to indications given in his correspondence with Theo, was probably painted in September 1889, when he was still in the hospital at Saint-Rémy, Van Gogh makes use of a striking monochrome field brought violently to life by undulating movements of the brush. The idea of a background carrying a strong emotional charge is typical of Van Gogh and very different from the sophisticated scene-setting of Gauguin. His approach to painting, so vital and authentic, explains the universality of Van Gogh's message. He gave this picture to his friend Dr Gachet, and was to commit suicide a year later.

CF-T

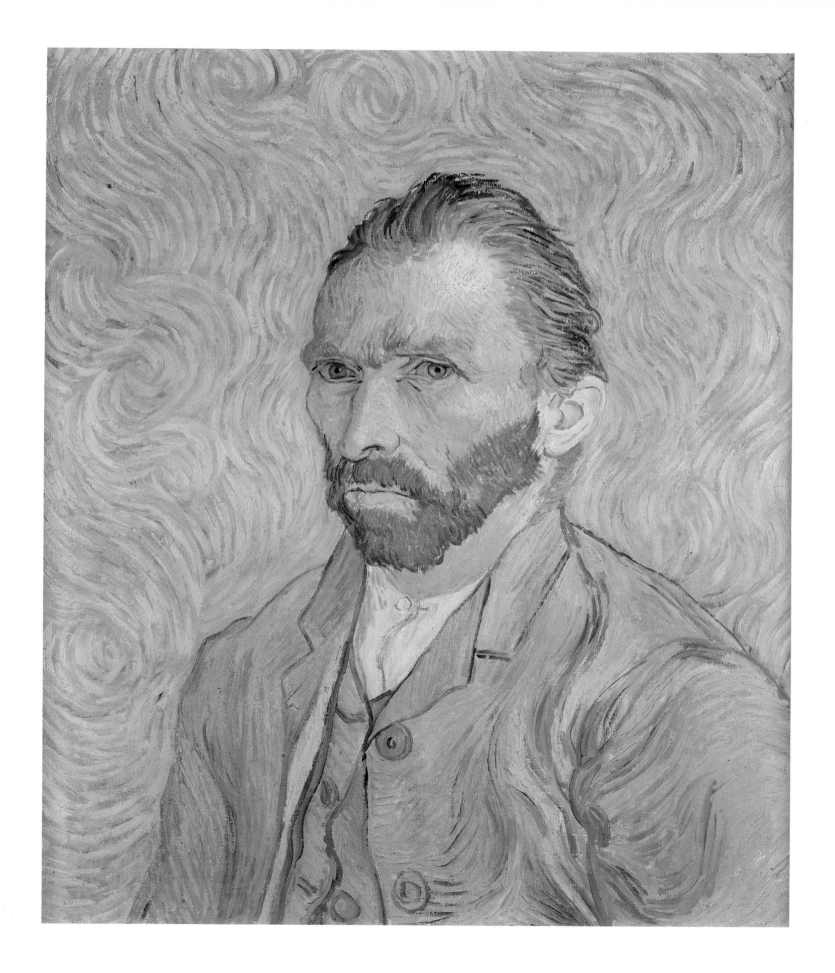

Vincent VAN GOGH (1853–1890)

La chambre de Van Gogh à Arles
(Van Gogh's Room at Arles), 1889

Oil on canvas, $22\frac{1}{2} \times 29\frac{1}{3}$ (57 × 74)

Former Matsukata Collection. Ceded to the Louvre under the terms of the peace treaty with Japan, 1959 (R.F. 1959–2)

La chambre de Van Gogh à Arles is perhaps the best-known of Van Gogh's paintings. It admits us into the painter's intimacy, but only partly reveals his secret. Full of blazingly discordant colour, this room is, with its rustic simplicity and bareness, the one which the painter occupied at Arles in the year 1888. Van Gogh made several drawings of it, and also three versions in oil, the first one in October 1888, followed by two copies (the painting in the Jeu de Paume is one of these) in September the following year. He speaks of it several times in his letters to Theo.

Van Gogh had dreamed of creating around himself a true artistic community – the famous 'Studio of the Midi' – and had persuaded Gauguin to come to live with him. But the stormy relationship between the two men inevitably deteriorated rapidly, and it was here that the famous incident took place – when, in the grip of a fit of madness, Van Gogh attacked his friend and afterwards cut off his own ear. The following spring, Van Gogh committed himself to the Hospice of Saint-Paul at Saint-Rémy, and there painted this picture. 'I'm working with a will in my room. It does me good and chases away my imaginings, my abnormal ideas', he wrote to Theo in September 1889. The picture is thus the radiant testimony of a man then confirmed to a madhouse, but also, as a retrospective view of his room at Arles, was done as an act of exorcism by someone for whom painting was truly therapeutic. The strident colours, which bear little relationship to reality, the shaky perspective, and the yawning void which fills this paradoxically tidy room, together create a painting which is enormously evocative. Its freedom of inspiration also had a considerable influence on Matisse in his *Large Interiors*.

CF-T

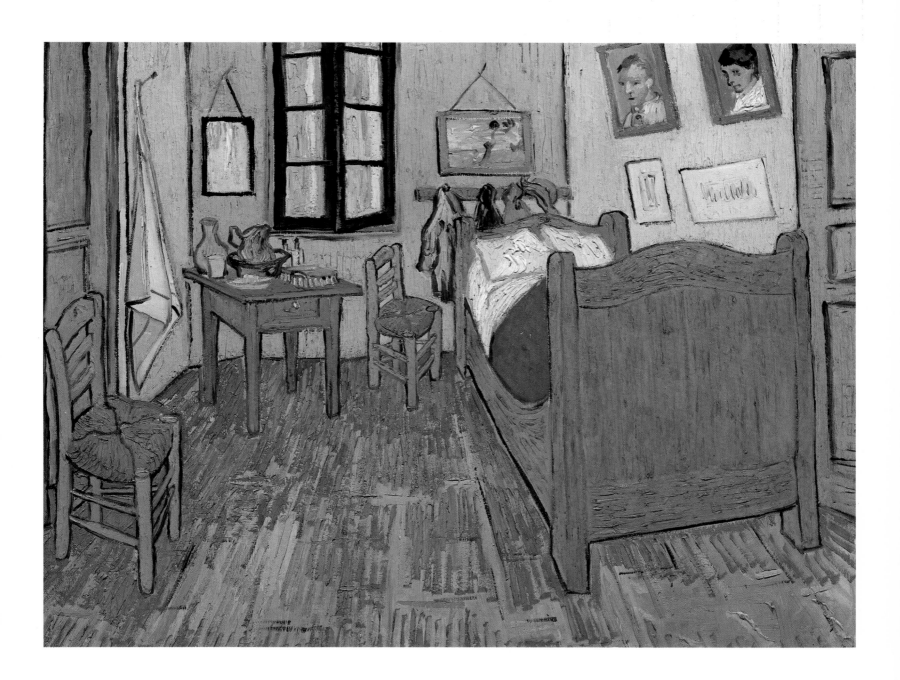

Vincent VAN GOGH (1853–1890)

La méridienne or *La sieste*

(*The Midday Nap* or *The Siesta*), 1889–90

Oil on canvas, $28\frac{3}{4} \times 35\frac{7}{8}$ (73 × 91)

Gift of Mme Fernand Halphen, but retained by her for her lifetime, 1952; entered the Jeu de Paume in 1963 (R.F. 1952–17)

Van Gogh nurtured an admiration for the work of certain artists, a fact which today we find somewhat disconcerting. For example, he held in esteem the work of his contemporaries Monticelli and Ziem, above all as colourists. But throughout his brief career he also profited greatly from the study of the Old Masters. He drew on Rubens, whom he was already copying in Antwerp in 1885–86, on Rembrandt and, nearer to his own time, on Delacroix (the *Pietà*, *Le Bon Samaritain*), on Gustave Doré (*La ronde des prisonniers*, or *Prisoners Walking in a Circle*), and on J. F. Millet, and took lessons from them. *La méridienne* is a copy after the second of a series of four drawings by Millet engraved by J. A. Lavieille, which represented 'Hours of the Day' in the life of a farm-worker: leaving for work, the midday nap, the end of the day and before bedtime. Hospitalized at Saint-Rémy, unable to paint from life because the state of his health was still precarious, Van Gogh worked on this painting in his room, during December 1889 and during 1890. 'I find this sort of thing teaches me something and above all consoles me', he wrote to Theo. 'Working thus on his drawings or on his woodcuts is not purely and simply copying. Rather it is translating into another language – that of colour – the impressions of light and shade in black and white.' This transcription, full of light, is based on a harmony of blue and yellow. The liveliness of the brush-strokes brings to life the marvellous harmony of lines and masses taken over from Millet. Van Gogh and Millet had always been linked by a common feeling for the dignity of the poor and for their universal value, and Millet inspired Van Gogh many times in the course of his career. Picasso drew on the same source during his classic period in 1919.   CF-T

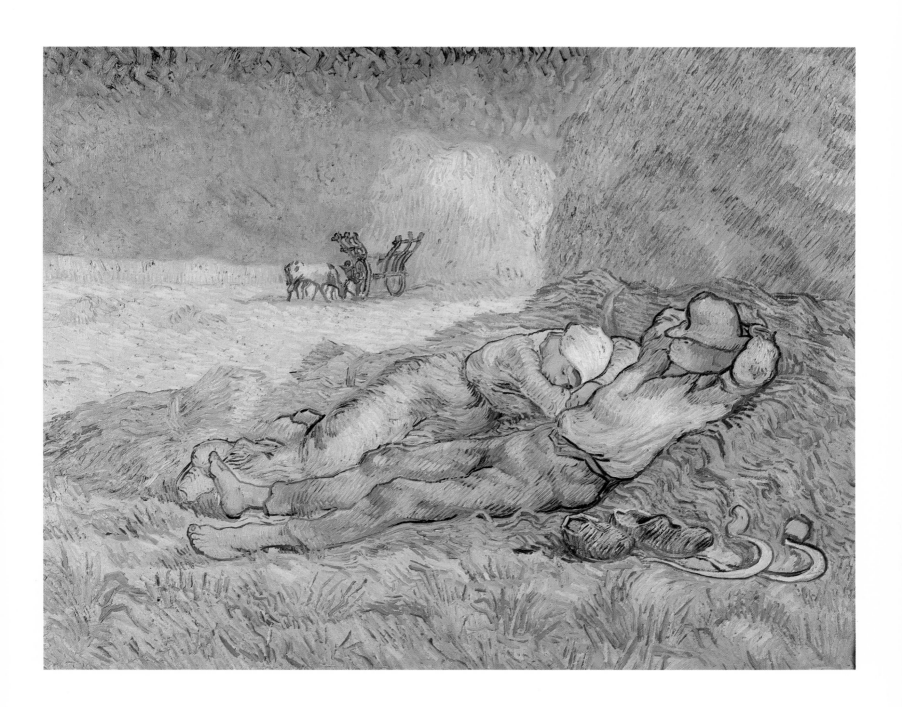

Vincent VAN GOGH (1853–1890)

Le docteur Paul Gachet, 1890

Oil on canvas, 26¾ × 22⅜ (68 × 57)

Gift of Paul and Marguerite Gachet, 1949 (R.F. 1949–15)

'What impassions me most – much, much more than all the rest of my métier – is the portrait, the modern portrait. I seek it in color, and surely I am not the only one to seek it in this direction. . . . *I should like* to paint portraits which would appear after a century to the people living then as apparitions', Van Gogh wrote to his sister Wilhelmina in June 1890. From this period comes the portrait of Dr Gachet, generously given – together with the self-portrait of 1889 – to the Jeu de Paume in 1949 by the sitter's children. After a brief stay in Paris, from 18 to 20 May, Van Gogh, now back on his feet again, went off to Auvers in the valley of the Oise. There he was made welcome by Dr Gachet. The valley itself was already a favoured spot with the Barbizon painters Daubigny, Corot and Dupré; others, such as Pissarro, Cézanne and Guillaumin, also worked there. And here the doctor, whose speciality was mental illness (he had published a treatise on melancholy), helped, with exceptional discernment and total disinterest, the painters who were also his friends. This man, 'incontestably the chief enthusiast for the new painting', as Gustave Cocquiot called him, provided Van Gogh with the last friendship of his dolorous career, and was to ease his last moments after the fatal self-inflicted wound. Gachet promised that 'if the melancholy or anything else became too much for me to bear, he could easily do something to lesson its intensity', wrote Van Gogh, who painted three poignantly expressive portraits of him.

The Gachet donation, made to the national collections by Dr Gachet's children and of which this painting is part, is one of the crowning glories of the Jeu de Paume. Here are shown side by side a number of masterpieces – paintings by Cézanne (*Une moderne Olympia*, p. 24, and *La maison du docteur Gachet*), Sisley, Renoir and Guillaumin, together with Van Gogh's final works, *Le jardin du docteur Gachet* and *L'église d'Auvers-sur-Oise* (p. 158).   CF-T

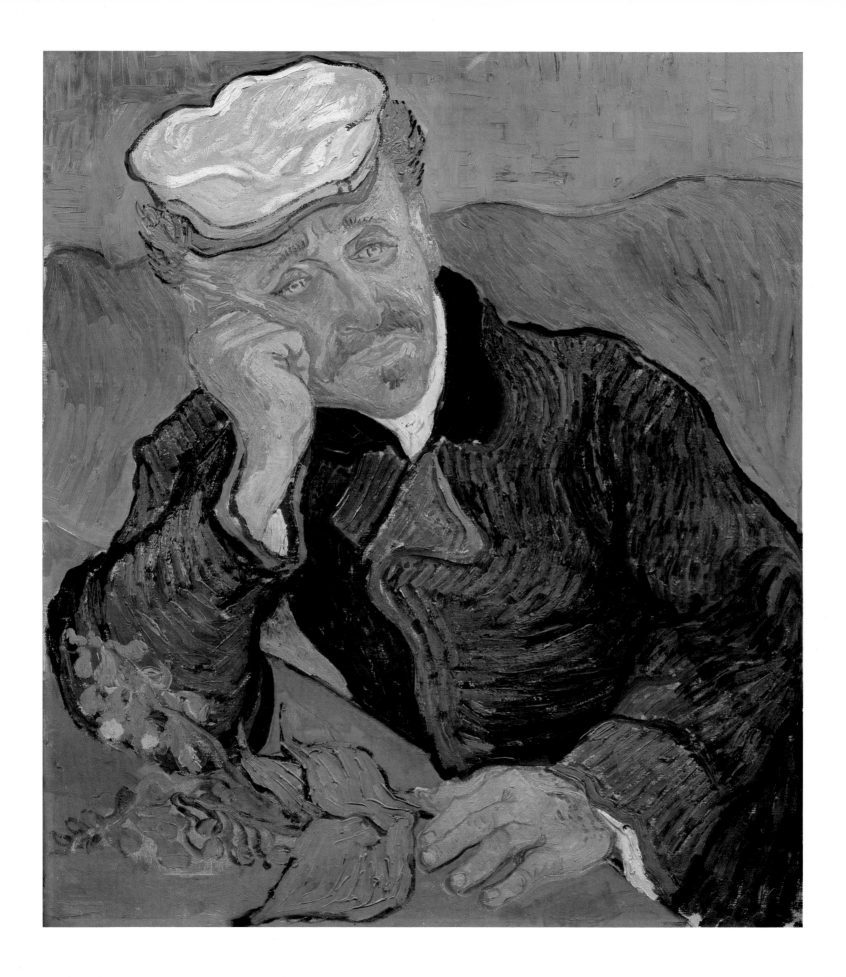

Vincent VAN GOGH (1853–1890)

L'église d'Auvers-sur-Oise (*The Church at Auvers-sur-Oise*), 1890

Oil on canvas, 37 × 29⅛ (94 × 74)

Purchased with the help of Paul Gachet and of an anonymous Canadian donation, 1951 (R.F. 1951–42)

'Here the faith of one man, maintained despite madness, maintained despite the menace of death, is equal to the fervour of the multitude', wrote André Malraux in 1952. The acquisition of *L'église d'Auvers* in 1951 provided the Jeu de Paume with one of the artist's final masterpieces. Van Gogh wrote about the picture to his sister, in a letter which can be dated between 4 and 8 June 1890: 'Apart from these I have a larger picture of the village church – an effect in which the building appears to be violet-hued against a sky of a simple deep blue colour, pure cobalt; the stained-glass windows appear as ultramarine blotches, the roof is violet and partly orange. In the foreground some green plants in bloom, and sand with the pink glow of sunshine on it. And once again it is nearly the same thing as the studies I did in Nuenen of the old tower and the cemetery, only it is probable that now the colour is more expressive, more sumptuous.' Van Gogh was to die two months later, on 29 July 1890. The animated silhouette of the church, seen looking towards the apse, appears against a brilliantly blue sky which seems lit from within by an intense mystical fervour. All the energy of the picture is concentrated into a last uprush of colour, punctuated by lively brush-strokes here and there in the foreground. The figure of the little peasant girl rapidly brushed in to the left symbolizes perhaps the trivial nature of everyday events. Very different from the Monet of the cathedrals which can be admired in a neighbouring room, this painting comes close to the nocturnal visions which were soon to be orchestrated by Expressionists such as Munch and Kirchner, or by Mondrian and Kandinský at the beginning of their careers. CF-T